TRANSITIONS

TRANSITIONS

A Guide to Transitioning for Transsexuals and Their Families

Mara Christine Drummond

Transitions
A Guide to Transitioning for Transsexuals and Their Families

Library of Congress Control Number: 2009902127

ISBN-13: 978-0-557-05261-5

To Sarah Zietlow and Mellissa Dyer, the two most
accepting people I have ever known.
I will never be able to thank you
enough for welcoming me into your lives.

CONTENTS

ACKNOWLEDGEMENTS

My transition would never have been a success were it not for the love, advice, assistance and talents of many people.

I can never repay Catherine Coulson, LCSW-C, for all the support and advice she has given my family and me over the years. In addition, my warmest appreciations go to Dr. Susan Fishbein, Psy. D., whose sound words of advice helped me overcome the major emotional challenges that constantly arose as I transitioned.

I would have never learned to speak properly without the loving instruction of Mary Elizabeth (Tish) Moody, MA, CCC-SLP, who was a friend, an unofficial counselor and an excellent speech therapist all rolled up into one. Thank you so, so much Tish!

The incredible kindnesses of Mary Della-Davis, LE, and Patty Peters BSN, RN, RE, made the many hours of electrolysis just slip right on by. Thank you both for being such wonderful people.

I am eternally indebted to my two surgeons, Dr. Douglas K. Ousterhout, MD, DDS, and Dr. Toby R. Meltzer, MD, PC, each of whom used his incredible talents to give me the face, body and life I dreamed of for over four decades. You are both truly incredible surgeons. I am truly incapable of expressing the gratitude that I feel for the inner peace and joy that has come to my life as a result of the changes you made to my face and body. Thank you so much for all that you have given me!

Special thanks to Mary-Lou and Tricia from the Cocoon House, and the nursing staffs of the California Pacific Medical Center, Davies Campus, and the Scottsdale Healthcare Greenbaum Surgery Center for all the love and care they gave me before and after my surgeries. I will never forget all that each of you did to help me survive the hardest days of my life.

Most importantly, I wish to thank my parents, my brother, my sisters, my daughters and my many, many friends, who all showed me incredible love and support throughout my entire transition. Thank you all for being such wonderful and caring people. I am truly blessed to have such wonderful people in my life.

Lastly, I would never have been able to publish this book without the feedback given to me by many people. To each of you who took the time to read the early versions of my work, thank you. I believe special recognition should be given to Maryanne Arnow, Lori Mull and Robin Sawyer, who each donated considerable time to help correct the many misuses of the English language that plagued earlier versions of this book. Both the readers and I thank you very much!

PREFACE

There are some statements in life that once said can never be unsaid. Saying "I think I'm transsexual." is probably right there on the top of the list right next to "I have been sleeping with your sister." So once you declare to that first person or to yourself that you are transsexual, you start down a long, dark road, a road that has many hairpin turns and unknown hazards along the way, possibly without any sense of where you are truly heading. The journey that you then undertake may be one of the hardest passages you will ever make.

Transitioning from one physical gender to another is an incredibly hard, confusing, complex, expensive and potentially devastating undertaking. I have fully experienced transitioning myself, and I have many friends whom I have watched or assisted in some way as they painfully made their own way through this most difficult process.

I decided to write this book after meeting an incredible number of transsexual people who were confused about how to successfully transition, who were facing possible rejection from family, or who stalled in the midst of their transitions. After spending a lot of time talking with them about their transition concerns, I realized there was no concise resource that helped explain what occurs as they undertake the incredible journey of a transition. *Transitions* grew out of that void.

Be advised though, that the information and advice I offer in this book is not science, nor is it based on any philosophy other than my own. I have not performed any formal studies, I do not have any degrees in psychology or psychiatry, and I do not belong to any professional psychiatric groups or institutions. I just learned incredible amounts about this process as I went through my own transition. My opinions and beliefs were born from all that I experienced and all that I learned from counselors, friends, families, political activism, internet sites, and support groups.

As you read this guide, please keep in mind that I do not wish to offend any person, group, or segment of society, but I cannot always be politically correct. So please excuse any prejudicial statements that you feel that I may have made. Transitioning has taught me to respect all people and all groups more than ever, but sometimes it not easy to say what needs to be said without possibly offending someone, somewhere.

If you identify as female-to-male, please excuse any tendency I have to use male-to-female subjects in many of my examples. I chose to do this in many instances solely for consistency and ease of reading. Unless stated otherwise, the advice I offer in this guide applies equally to both male-to-female and female-to-male transgender people.

If you are considering changing your gender, I hope this guide will help prepare you for the incredible demands of a gender transition. I hope that the issues and concerns raised in this guide will help you carefully weigh all the consequences and benefits a transition may bring to your life before you embark upon a journey similar to mine. Most importantly, I hope that you find a way to bring peace and happiness to your life.

If you are a family member or friend of a person who is undergoing a change of gender, I hope this guide helps you understand the feelings you may experience as you watch this person whom you care for so much change his or her life so radically. I hope you develop an understanding of what drives someone to make such a major change in his or her life. I hope you come to understand the hardships that are taken on when someone decides to transition. Most of all, though, I hope you learn enough from this guide to be able to continue to love and support this special person, before, during, and after his or her transition, if that is the path taken to find inner peace and happiness.

– Mara

COMING TO TERMS

Throughout my transition, I had several great experiences speaking at colleges and universities. What I learned early on is that the majority of people have heard of the terms transgender, transsexual, gay, lesbian, sexual orientation, and such, but they truly do not have a clue as to what these terms actually mean. Even people in the lesbian, gay, bi-sexual and transgender (LGBT) communities do not always understand the differences between these terms, and often there is much confusion and misunderstanding. Therefore, I adopted a habit of briefly explaining the terms I was going to be using as I spoke. I made sure that I always explained these terms as the very first thing I did even if it initially may have offended some members of the group to which I was talking.

I tried the best I could to use definitions that I felt were easy to understand but that does not mean that everyone has the same definitions that I use. Having the perfect definition for each term is not a critical requirement. It is critical, however, that everyone with whom you communicate understands these terms in the sense with which you use them. If they do not, you may just be confusing them and possibly be causing them to make prejudicial judgments about you.

Listed below are terms I feel are important to clarify. These could be in an appendix at the back, but it is critically important that you fully understand these key terms before going any further in this book.

Gender Identity: The innate (inborn) sense of gender that a person feels internally. A person's sense of gender may or may not be harmonious with his or her physical gender. Everyone has a gender identity although the vast majority of people may not realize it as being a separate aspect of their being due to their gender identity being congruent with their physical gender.

Sex (Physical Gender): The classification of people as male or female based on each person's genitalia, genetic makeup, hormones, and internal reproductive organs.

Sexual orientation: The sexual attraction that a person feels towards another person based on the gender of the other person. Sexual orientation is a human characteristic unique and distinct from gender identity. While gender identity is about one's own sense of gender, sexual orientation is about one's attraction to someone else because of that other person's gender.

Incongruent Gender Identity: Having a sense of gender that is incompatible with one's physical gender characteristics.

Transgender: An umbrella term that covers any person who has a gender identity that is incongruous in any way with his or her sex. Included under the transgender umbrella are people who feel discomfort expressing themselves as a member of their own gender (e.g. butch women or effeminate men). Also included are people who sometimes wear the attire of the other gender (e.g. cross-dressers), and those who feel they are a mixture of genders[1] (i.e. gender androgynous). At the extremes, the term transgender takes in people who feel they are not of any gender (i.e. gender neutral), and people who want to live their lives in a manner consistent with the gender opposite their birth sex (i.e. transsexuals).

Transsexual: A person who has a gender identity that is opposite his or her birth sex, and who strongly feels he or she should live fully as a member of the gender with which he or she identifies. Hence, a transsexual is either a genetic man who lives as a woman, or a genetic woman who lives as a man. A person does not have to surgically alter his or her gender to be transsexual. A person who lives his or her life as

---

[1] Gender androgynous and gender neutral are two sub-categories of the people who identify as genderqueer or intergendered. Genderqueer is a gender identity of both, neither, or some combination of male and / or female.

a member of the opposite gender without ever undergoing or planning to undergo surgery is a non-operative (non-op) transsexual. A person who is preparing to undergo gender reassignment surgery is a pre-operative (pre-op) transsexual. A person who has undergone gender reassignment surgery is a post-operative (post-op) transsexual[2]. For females who make the transition to male, reassignment surgery of the genitals is not always an effective or desired medical procedure. Surgical removal of the breasts is often the criteria used to judge whether a transsexual man is pre- or post-operative.

Transwoman: A transgender person who was born male, and who identifies and portrays her gender as female. Other terms for transwoman are male-to-female and MTF.

Transman: A transgender person who was born female, and who identifies and portrays his gender as male. Other terms for transman are female-to-male and FTM.

Gay: A man or transman who has a sexual orientation in which the sexual attraction focuses upon other men.

Lesbian: A woman or transwoman who has a sexual orientation in which the sexual attraction focuses upon other women.

Bi-sexual: A person who has a sexual orientation in which there is sexual attraction towards members of both sexes.

Cross-dresser: Anyone who dresses in clothing not associated with his or her assigned sex; generally refers to a male who dresses as

---

[2] Some post-operative transsexuals take offense when people refer to them as transsexual once they have completely undergone all the surgical procedures required to physically transition from one gender to the other. They prefer to be classified as simply men or women. I will not argue whether they are right or wrong on this point, but defining the term post-op transsexual is required because it is so often used.

female, who may or may not desire to change his gender; considered more politically correct than the term "transvestite."

Transvestite: Typically used to describe a male who dresses as a female, often for sexual gratification reasons. This term tends to draw disapproval when used to reference to a transgender person.

Making sense of these terms is not always an easy task for some, possibly most, people. For instance, the majority of people simply have a gender identity that has always been unquestionably congruous with their birth sex. Inasmuch, the first time they hear the term "gender identity" used, they do not even comprehend that it is possible for someone to have a permanent sense of gender that is opposite or different from his or her physical sex.

People also often confuse gender identity and sexual orientation, thinking that these two terms mean the same thing. Always make sure that anyone with whom you discuss gender identity issues understands that gender identity is about one's own sense of gender while sexual orientation is about one's attraction to another based on the other person's gender.

A STARTING POINT

Being transgender is not something a person just wakes up one day and decides to become. Transgender people typically go through life with feelings that their gender identity is inconsistent with their physical gender characteristics. These feelings are distinct from the self-realization that one is transgender or transsexual, and may cause them to act, speak, dress, or socialize in a manner that does not correspond in part or at all with their birth sex.

For example, let us say a young boy has been attempting to present himself as a girl on a regular basis. He is not aware that he has an issue with his gender identity and correspondingly he does not know he is transgender; he just instinctively tries to dress and do things like girls his age.

Depending upon his age, though, he may have a strong internal belief that he is physically a girl, or, if he is old enough to understand the basic differences between the sexes, he may believe he was mistakenly born as a boy and want to change into a girl. If the feelings he experiences are consistent and present on a continuing basis, not just feelings of a passing curiosity, the child has an incongruent gender identity, more often referred to as a Gender Identity Disorder[3] (GID). If the feelings this boy is experiencing causes him anxiety, unease, or

---

[3] The mental health profession classifies the condition of having a gender identity that is inconsistent with one's physical gender as a psychological disorder known as Gender Identity Disorder (GID). There is an ongoing effort to stop using GID as a mental health diagnosis. I agree with this effort and instead prefer using the term "incongruent gender identity" as it does not imply that the condition of having a gender identity that is inconsistent with one's sex is a psychological disorder.

depression, he is suffering the effects of what is clinically referred to as "gender dysphoria".

Generally speaking though, transgender people do not know that what they are feeling about their gender is wrong until someone points it out to them that they are not acting appropriately for their gender, or they learn on their own what society deems appropriate for each gender. Let's face it, society generally believes there are just two genders, male and female, each with its own set of associated behaviors, norms, and dress. Modern western society has not generally embraced the fact that there are gender variations beyond male or female. Society tends to ignore the fact that some people are born intersexed[4] and the fact that some people have gender identities that do not match their physical gender.

When a transgender person starts to realize that his or her gender identity is discordant with his physical gender, there develops within that person a level of discomfort. This level of discomfort may wax and wane throughout life. The way each individual copes with this discomfort generally results in a set of actions that are associated with the many different transgender classifications. For instance, when the discomfort level is low, a person may just act effeminately or tomboyish. When the discomfort level rises, the person may start cross-dressing[5] privately. If the discomfort continues to rise, the person may venture out in public cross-dressed on a limited basis. If the discomfort level becomes too great, the person may start to consider living as the other gender permanently. Hence, what really defines the different variations of the transgender spectrum is the

---

[4] Intersexed refers to people who's sex chromosomes, genitalia and / or secondary sex characteristics are determined to be neither purely male nor purely female.

[5] Cross-dressing is the act of wearing clothing appropriate for the other physical gender.

action that is required for a person to manage the discomfort caused by his or her gender identity incongruence.

Living one's life as the other gender, that is being a transsexual, is therefore just a remedy for the severe discomfort one feels about his or her gender identity in relation to his or her physical gender. If simply living one's life as a member of the other gender is sufficient to counteract this discomfort, then a person may remain a non-operative transsexual for as long as he or she can manage to keep the discomfort at a reasonable level. If a person feels that altering his or her physical gender to match his or her gender identity is the only way to eliminate the emotional discomfort being experienced, then the person is a pre- or post-operative transsexual.

If you understand that having an incongruent gender identity causes discomfort and the actions one takes are just ways of managing that discomfort, then it is easy to see how a person may initially cross-dress in private and years later become a transsexual. As the discomfort level rises, the response to the discomfort changes correspondingly. It is not always clear why the level of discomfort for some people rises to the level of wanting gender reassignment surgery while for others the level of discomfort stays manageable without surgery. It is important to note, however, that the discomfort level can reach a critical point for some people, and that the discomfort level change rate is unique for each affected person.

When the discomfort level gets to the critical point in which a person wants to have gender reassignment surgery, the unease and depression caused by being unable to obtain surgery or live in the desired gender may become so great as to generate a desire to hurt or kill oneself. Please seek immediate professional mental health care if you or someone you know is experiencing suicidal feelings brought on by being transgender or any other reason.

When you believe your level of discomfort between your physical gender and gender identity has reached the level where you want to physically alter your gender to that of the opposite sex, then it is time you start understanding all that you will be required to do to successfully accomplish this task.

INNER STRENGTH

Of all the concepts that you must learn in order to successfully transition, I firmly believe the most important is:

The only way to successfully transition is to accept the possibility that by transitioning you may lose everything of value in your life.

Let's be honest. Nobody wants to lose everything of value in his or her life. However, unless you are mentally prepared to accept the very real possibility that you may lose all or some of the things in your life that you hold sacred, you will either not be able to start transitioning, or you will stall somewhere in the middle of your transition. The fear of losing a spouse, custody of your children, your parents, siblings, friends, neighbors, home, employment, religious community, etc. can be extremely overwhelming or downright debilitating.

If your transition stalls, it may be months or years before conditions in your life change, or you gain the courage to carry on. I have heard countless people talk about their spouses threatening divorce and expressing their fears of being ejected from their homes if they continue transitioning. I have also heard time after time "I'm going to lose my job if my employer finds out," and "I'm going to look for another job soon, but for now I cannot let my boss know about this." Are you realistically going to be able to find another job that is accepting of your transition once you have started making physical changes, and if so, when and where?

Accepting the possibility that you may lose the most important things in your life is not the same thing as giving up hope. It is crucial that you do not give up hope that things will get better when all seems like it is going wrong.

Therefore, what I suggest here is that you find a very good therapist, preferably with gender identity specific training, someone with whom you can feel comfortable, and that you feel understands you and your situation. Start with a therapist earlier rather than later. If you do not necessarily believe your therapist fully understands you, keep searching for a therapist until you find someone you relate to very well.

I believe a good therapist will know almost immediately whether you are legitimately transsexual, and he or she will immediately start to focus on helping you get through the transition process if you are. If you are not truly transsexual, your therapist should help you manage your gender specific anxiety and depression in ways that do not include transitioning.

By offering you a way to face your fears, and by helping you determine how important transitioning to the other gender really is to you, your therapist may help you find the inner strength to overcome the fear of losing everything. On the other hand, with a therapist's help you may find before you come out and tell the world that you are transsexual, that you just cannot bring yourself to risk the loss of some of the things that you treasure most, such as your family or your home. You just may realize you must handle the stress caused by having an incongruent gender identity without transitioning to the other gender, or living full-time as the other gender.

When I walked into my therapist's office the first time, I was terrified. My therapist and I knew each other for six years prior to the day I sat down in her office for the first time as a patient. I still remember the sheer level of terror that I felt as I prepared to say, "I think I might be transsexual." This was so incredibly hard for me to do, but I had to do it nonetheless. What you will find when you start to transition, if you have not already, is that the entire transitioning process is filled with incredibly hard challenges that must be recognized, addressed, and then completed.

How do you tell your family and friends? How do you find other people like yourself? How do you survive the embarrassment of going out in public cross-dressed when you do not pass very well as a member of the gender with which you identify? How do you explain the plucked eyebrows, manicured nails or bound breasts to your employer when they ask why you look different? Can you answer your daughter when she asks, "Mommy, why do you look like a boy?" in front of your neighbors? There are so many obstacles and challenges along the transition path; you may sometimes feel you will never overcome them all.

Much inner strength is required to overcome these and all the other challenges that present themselves to you as you transition. As very few people are capable of prevailing over so many challenges entirely on their own, you will most likely need many people – friends, family, counselors, support groups, etc. – to gain and maintain the inner strength needed to complete your transition. Insomuch, you should constantly be seeking new avenues of support to conquer the challenges that you face change.

If you cannot find a local support group, I recommend making the effort of joining one in the nearest large urban area even if that means you have to drive a couple of hours to get there. Do not substitute an online chat group or message board for a real support group. Do not get me wrong, chat groups and message boards are great resources at times, but they cannot compare to having the personal, face-to-face interactions found only in live support groups.

Personally, I initially did not think I needed a support group to help me with my transition. My therapist would suggest time after time that I attend a local support group meeting. I was too proud to think I needed the help of a support group. When I started to realize that I may actually be able to physically transition, I caved in and started to attend a support group so I could "data mine" it, that is, to find out which doctors and which therapists were best for transitioning purposes in my area. What I unexpectedly found was how wonderful the people who attended the group were, and how much care, kindness, support and knowledge they were willing to offer me. Now, some of my very best friends are the other members of the groups I have joined.

As you start to transition, you will find transitioning is not just about changing your body to match your gender identity. Transitioning also requires you to learn how to live fully as a member of the gender with which you identify, not just "be" a member of the gender with which you identify. The physical changes that you make are just some of the mechanics needed to reduce the discomfort and unease that come along with a change of gender.

Anyone with a decent income could save enough money to pay a surgeon to alter his or her genitals and face to match the opposite gender. However, successfully living as a member of the opposite gender for the rest of your life takes an incredible amount of effort, inner strength, and commitment. Do not lie to yourself and think you can do this alone and without support. You may just be going down a rabbit hole from which you cannot escape. There is a reason why the suicide rate among pre-op transsexuals is so high. Think about it...

SELF-ACCEPTANCE

I have a personal theory that therapists help people with gender identity disorders primarily in three ways. Initially they assist by helping someone with an incongruent gender identity accept who they are. Then they provide guidance and expertise to help overcome the anxiety and fears caused by both coming out[6] to family, friends, coworkers, etc., and by living in a new gender role. Finally, therapists teach transsexuals to cope with the sadness and disappointment that arise when others fail to fully accept them in their new gender.

I am sure there will be many other things your therapist may do to assist in your transition, such as providing referral letters and helping you resolve other issues that come up as you transition. However, I believe the three areas listed above are the primary areas for which you should be seeking and getting the most assistance from your therapist.

Self-acceptance is more than just acknowledging to yourself that you are transsexual. True self-acceptance occurs when you realize that you are a good, decent human being even though one of your personal attributes is a gender identity / physical gender mismatch. If you cannot accept yourself as being the wonderful person I hope you are, then you will never be able to convince someone else to accept you. You will never gain the self-confidence to go out in public outside of the LGBT community. And you will never have the strength to fight for your rights if someone tries to trample them.

---

[6] Coming out is when a person discloses to someone else that she or he is transgender or transsexual.

In order to accept yourself, you have to accept that being gender variant does not diminish you in any way. Being gender variant in my opinion is a plus, not a minus. Having lived as a man while having the feelings of a woman deep down inside may have allowed you to experience the world from a male perspective while reacting with the empathy, care and love that is typically associated with being a woman. It is truly the best of all worlds. The same holds true for the many transmen who bring to their male worlds what they have learned growing up as females. Sure, it is tough to have an incongruent gender identity. Surely, there are going to be people who look down upon those who are transgender or transsexual. Nevertheless, you, as the transsexual, must consciously realize that being transsexual is a positive attribute of your personality and not have any shame about being transsexual.

Gaining this kind of self-acceptance is not easy to do. Depending upon your age, you may have endured decades of negative stereotyping about transgender people and transsexuals. How many times did family or society try to drill into you how wrong it is to not follow the expected gender norms? How can you be a good person and still violate the gender based expectations and requirements of the society or culture that you live in?

The answers to these questions and the solution to finding self-acceptance are to realize that your gender identity problem is simply a product of pre-natal or early childhood development[7], not a deviant sexual fantasy[8] as some wrongly suggest, and is a basic healthcare issue that requires resolution. There cannot be self-acceptance if you view

---

[7] There are numerous theories on what causes an incongruent gender identity, but no single theory of causation has been proven beyond a doubt.

[8] A subset of people dress in the other gender's clothing for purposes of sexual arousal or as a form of sexual fetish. There is a trend to refer to people who dress for either of these reasons as transvestites, and those who cross-dress due to an incongruent gender identity as cross-dressers.

an incongruent gender identity as being morally or socially wrong. Having a gender identity that does not match your sex is not a condition that can be self-induced or learned. Your gender identity is set once it forms, and you are not going to change it. The mental health community has tried for years to "reset" transsexuals' gender identities to no avail; hence, the only health care solution at present is for medical intervention that alters the physical gender of transsexuals to match their gender identities.

Do not be surprised if your self-acceptance seems to decrease at various times in your transition. It is extremely hard to be proud of yourself when someone is staring at you because you are a transwoman and you have a 5 o'clock shadow, or you are a transman and your breasts are too big. It is hard to maintain your self-acceptance when someone you love and hold dear to your heart rejects you, calls you a nasty name, or abandons you. Inner strength and self-acceptance go hand-in-hand. You have to have the inner strength to maintain your own self-acceptance in the face of rejection and discrimination from others.

So how do you learn to accept yourself? Speak with a therapist who understands you, and who understands that an incongruent gender identity is neither a perversion nor morally wrong. Talk with loved ones or good friends whom you trust and who respect you as a person. Read and learn about gender identity disorders and their suspected causes. Join a support group and meet new friends who appreciate you regardless of how you present yourself. Go to a nightclub or bar in the LGBT-friendly section of town, and talk with non-transgender people. My own self-acceptance grew an incredible amount as I met people in LGBT-friendly bars who saw me for the person I am, and not as the person whom I used to be.

It is critical you understand that being transsexual does not define you as a person. Being transsexual is just one of your many traits, that when combined, help to more clearly define you as a whole person.

If you want to get philosophical for a moment, put together a list of people whom you believe think highly of you, who believe you to be a good person, and who do not know you are transsexual. Now that you have your list, how is it that these people still think so highly of you? You are transsexual whether they know it or not, but they still think you are a good person.

If they do not know you are transsexual, but immediately reject you when you tell them, is it because the disclosure that you are transsexual instantaneously changed you from a good person to a bad person? Of course not! Their negative reaction is a change within *them*. *They* changed their opinions of you in response to their own internal prejudices and beliefs. The only change *you* underwent was the emotional impact caused by their rejections, but you are still fundamentally the same person. So, if you were a good person before you disclosed you are transsexual, how can you not be a good person after you disclosed you are transsexual if you have not undergone any change other than having your feelings hurt?

If you think long enough about this, you will understand. Therapists, family, and friends just help to reinforce that you are a good person, and hence, they make it easier for you to accept yourself.

COMING OUT

Unlike people with same-sex or bi-sexual sexual orientations that wish to live their lives with their sexual orientation hidden, a transsexual person usually cannot live as the opposite gender without others finding out. The world around you will definitely notice and react the first time the "new" you appears on the scene. Without proper education and explanation, a chance encounter with the "new" you may completely destroy the relationship you have with a family member or friend. Therefore, transsexuals must go through a process of disclosing to just about everyone they know in their lives that they have incongruent gender identities, are now living or will be living as the opposite gender, and whether or not they will be physically transitioning to the other gender. This disclosure process is commonly referred to "coming out," which is an abbreviated form of "coming out of the closet."

The coming out period is a very emotional time for most transsexuals. There exists a risk that someone or many of the people whom you tell will not support you after you come out to them. They may reject you, and they may choose to leave your life. For this reason, incredibly high levels of anxiety and unease often accompany the coming out period. If someone whom you truly care for rejects you, you may fall victim to situational depression. Having proper support through this period of your life is critical. If there is ever a time during your transition that you will truly need the help of a therapist, this is probably it. Coming out is part of the anxiety stage of therapy that was mentioned earlier.

Please seek professional assistance before you start coming out to people. As I stated on the first line of the preface, some things in life cannot be unsaid. Having a confirmation from a therapist that you are truly transsexual and not just one of the other transgender variants is an important fact you should know before you start to tell everyone you are transsexual. If you truly are not transsexual and will not be living as the opposite gender, there may be no reason to tell anyone of your incongruent gender identity. It is your reputation, your family, and your friendships that are at risk. Do not risk destroying them accidentally or unnecessarily if possible.

The goal of coming out is to prevent being rejected, abandoned or discriminated against by those whom surround you in life. You accomplish this goal by teaching others about your incongruent gender identity and your plans for transitioning. How you go about teaching them, though, is more of an art than it is a science. I learned a lot over the twenty-month period during which I came out, and what follows is mostly what I learned from this process. I consider myself very lucky as I lost so few people whom I cared for in the transition process. My therapist says this is not luck but the product of a lot of planning and effort on my part. I still feel very lucky, though, even if she is right.

One of the first things I discovered was that the majority of people have no idea what an incongruent gender identity is; what a transgender person is; what a transsexual is; or how "trans" anything is different from "being gay". As the media creates more and more programs that show transgender people in a positive light, education of the population is slowly occurring. However, you can never assume that the person you are talking to clearly understands all of the terms you will be using when you talk with them. So make sure you are prepared to explain the key terms you will be using. If possible, define the terms you will be using before you get too deep into your conversation to prevent them from making the wrong conclusions about you early on in this discussion.

It is very possible that no matter what your relationship is with the person you are about to tell, unless you are obviously effeminate or butch in your daily life, he or she is probably going to be shocked at your disclosure. Most people never entertain the possibility that a relative or friend of theirs really wants to live as the opposite gender, become a member of the opposite gender; or as they see it, "Oh my God, have a sex change!" When you tell them, they will likely be shocked. This was true for everyone who knew me when I came out. I only know of one person who, ahead of time, figured out on her own that I might be transsexual.

Each person to whom you come out will react in a unique manner. Do not even try to predict each person's response. You will just be wasting your time. Each person evaluates your disclosure using a very broad range of criteria, several of which may be very deeply rooted and hidden from general view. Here are some of the factors that influence people's reactions.

Respect: If the person you are coming out to respects you, he or she will have much more tolerance for accommodating you in your hour of need. Do not underestimate how much people are willing to overlook or ignore when they have respect or great love for you. On the other hand, if you lived your life as an ass all the way up to the point of coming out, do not be shocked when people consider that this latest thing you are doing is "one thing too many" as they toss you aside.

Empathy: A person will be much more tolerant of your situation if you connect with them on an emotional basis when you come out to them. You cannot just tell a factual story that does not relay the emotional journey of being transsexual. The story needs to contain a human element that discloses whatever hurt and angst you have felt throughout your life. An empathetic listener will be far more understanding than one who cannot relate to you on a personal level. Expect a bad response if your story is purely factual. A purely factual story requires the listener to determine on his own what emotional impact you are feeling or felt. Do not expect or let others do that. They may come to the wrong conclusion.

Religion: When it comes to religious arguments, just accept from the start that you are not going to win a theological argument or change a person's religious beliefs. What you can do, though, is educate a religious person on what an incongruent gender identity is. You can try to explain how your gender identity disorder has created great problems in your life, and how you believe God would want you to solve those problems. Probably the most important thing you can do, however, is to explain how an incongruent gender identity is not the same as homosexuality. Many religious people often wrongly apply to transsexuals the hate they feel towards homosexuality due to their inability to distinguish between gender identity and sexual orientation. They may also wrongly assume that their own beliefs towards transsexuals, transsexuality, and gender change are the official policies of their religion. You might benefit greatly by finding out in advance of your meeting the official policies of their religion with regards to gender identity, transsexuality and gender reassignment so that you can enlighten them if need be.

Family Impact: A subset of people exists whose primary concern will be the impact your transition will have on your family. Do not discount the concerns they raise. Because they love the members of your family, they really do worry about what will happen to each member of your family. They may relate to, love, and care for your family more than they care for you. If someone brings up a family impact issue, the focus of the issue will almost certainly be on the impact your transition will have on your spouse and children if you are married, or in a civil union or committed same-sex relationship. What they tell you will probably be the truth for the majority of spouses (more about this later); however, the impact on the children is an area that they are probably guessing at more often than not. Since your spouse/partner deserves to be the first person to know of your plans to transition after you obtain affirmation from your therapist that you are transsexual, you should have a good understanding of how your spouse/partner is reacting to your plans, and you should have a good sense of whether your relationship will survive before you talk with other people. Be honest with your listener. Show compassion for and be compassionate to those in your family whom your transition will negatively affect. If possible, try to educate your listener within the realm of what you and your spouse/partner feel comfortable disclosing about how you plan to minimize the impact on your family.

Experiences: If the person to whom you are coming out had a bad encounter in the past with someone he or she believed to be transgender or transsexual, he or she may show you negative bias. Negative bias may also arise from television shows (the "Jerry Springer" effect) or movies (e.g. *The Crying Game*) the person has seen. To fight a negative bias, you need to determine the cause of the bias. Then you must face the daunting task of either re-educating the person you are coming out to, or proving you are nothing like the person he or she encountered or saw in the media. The person he or she encountered or saw on TV may have been a transvestite, a drag queen[9], or someone without a gender problem just trying to get undeserved attention. You have to be very clear that you intend to live and present yourself as a decent woman or man, not as a freak, and certainly not as he or she imagines you to be. You may have to enumerate the steps you are going to take to be normal and fit in when you transition. If you present well and are not presenting when you make your disclosure, offer the person the opportunity to see the "new" you, so he or she can visually differentiate you from the negative image they possess.

Gender Bias: There seems to be a bias that arises when one "leaves the pack" sexually speaking. Part of this is due to society's gender norms and the resulting separation of the genders that occurs due to these norms. Because of this gender bias, people of your birth gender most likely will feel they can no longer communicate with you as they previously did. They may also be revolted at your desire to change your gender as they may see your transition as a criticism of their own gender. On the other hand, people of the gender you are transitioning to may seem to be much more accepting as you are becoming like them, becoming one of them. They may have a "welcome to the tribe" mentality that fosters better communication between you and them.

---

[9] A drag queen is generally a gay male who dresses as a woman for entertainment purposes. A drag queen does not generally have any desire to change genders and is generally comfortable with his birth gender.

Loss of friendship: When you announce your decision to transition, your existing friends may possibly feel they can no longer be friends of yours because they wrongly believe that you will no longer have an interest in the things you shared in common for so long. For instance, if you are a transwoman, and you and your male friend shared a common interest in sports, woodworking, etc., he may feel that because you are becoming a woman you will no longer want to participate in any of these activities in the future. He may feel rejected since he feels the two of you will no longer have anything in common. Inasmuch, he thinks he is losing a friend due to your transition. Prevent this from happening by letting your friends know that you are still the same person with the same interests and loves. Yes, there may be some changes in interests and activities over time, but if you think that in the future you will still love doing the things with your friends that you did with them in the past, make sure they know this. Then find the time to be a friend to the people you call your friends.

Judgmental: A subset of people believes that altering your body to correct what they perceive to be a mental defect[10] or "lifestyle" issue is wrong. I believe the best way you can handle this argument is by stressing the fact that there is no effective mental health solution to your gender dysphoria and that you are not making a lifestyle choice by trying to relieve yourself of the pain brought on by your incongruent gender identity. Explain that the gender dysphoria you experience has reached a level you can no longer bear, and therefore, you are taking the only possible steps known to alleviate the mental anguish you experience as a result of having an incongruent gender identity. Let them know you cannot imagine anyone wishing to undergo such drastic life changes and body modifications unless there truly exists no

---

[10] Unfortunately, the mental health community still classifies Gender Identity Disorder as a mental health diagnosis in the DSM-IV TR manual. Although there is a strong push by psychiatrists and psychologists to get this classification removed, at this time you are technically considered to have a mental defect if you have an incongruent gender identity.

other option that can help them find inner peace. Be forewarned that judgmental people often hold true to their own beliefs, as if their beliefs were a religion.

Suck it up and suffer: Some people will believe that if you are older and / or married that you should just "suck it up and suffer" so that your family and friends do not have to deal with the emotional damage your transition will cause in their lives. What these people fail to realize is that the level of distress caused by having an incongruent gender identity has reached a level that you can no longer manage without transitioning. You need to explain to them how your level of distress has become greater with age. Let them know how you feel (and hopefully your therapist agrees) and that you can no longer use the methods that you used earlier in life to suppress the mental anguish. Do not be surprised if the argument that you make does not sway them, especially if they are of the mindset that heaven is the reward for suffering through life.

The solutions I suggest for handling the problems that arise when you come out to someone are just suggestions. If a suggestion that I make does not fit your situation, do not lie and tell someone what you think he or she wants to hear just because I suggested it. Be honest and earn the respect of those to whom you come out. People hate a liar, and if they catch you lying, everything else you say to them will be suspect.

I took the approach during my coming out period that I would answer anyone's questions honestly and to the best of my ability regardless of how hard or personal those questions were. Be forewarned that the answers to personal questions, however, can cause very strong emotional responses in both you and in the person you are coming out to. I believe, though, that being honest in this manner builds respect for you as an individual, helps the other person understand the full emotional impact of what you have experienced, and helps establish a stronger emotional bond between you and the other person.

I have taken this approach with just about everyone I have talked with regarding my transition. As I result, I believe I have not lost friendships I thought would be lost. Instead, I have formed new and stronger friendships by being honest and frank with those I have encountered on my journey.

SPOUSES AND PARTNERS

Explaining what I have learned about coming out to spouses or partners is not easy to accept. If you are in a marriage or long- term same-sex relationship, be prepared to do some serious reflection on what is important to you after you have read this section.

When you transition and change your physical gender, you are indirectly asking that your spouse or partner change their sexual orientation. **To be blunt, this is not a reasonable thing to do. A person's sexual orientation is set in them just as much as your gender identity is set in you.** You cannot reasonably expect that your heterosexual spouse is going to want to be in a same sex relationship, or have family and friends view her or him as being either lesbian or gay. If you and your partner are in a same-sex relationship before you transition, the same holds true. You cannot expect your partner to want to be in a heterosexual relationship after your transition. This just is not a fair expectation for you to make, no matter how you slice it, dice it, or roll it.

One of the key factors that your spouse or partner considered when deciding to be in a marriage or long-term relationship with you was your physical gender. Do not be naïve and think he or she became your partner just for your brain, wit, humor, or thoughtfulness. The odds are very strong that your physical gender provides some foundation for your partner's sexual attraction to you, and subconsciously influences the way the two of you interact with each other. You cannot reasonably expect that your partner will want to continue to have sexual relations, or for that matter, even be seen as being intimately involved with you, when you are presenting as the other gender. There are exceptions to this rule, but for most heterosexual couples this rule is pretty firm.

I have come to believe that the only marriages that survive for a transsexual following a transition are those marriages that are purely platonic, or in which the non-transitioning spouse has strong bi-sexual or same-sex feelings. This does not imply an average heterosexual spouse will not conclude that his or her marriage is worth saving even though his or her spouse is changing gender. Maybe he or she will think it is an improvement. I am just expressing an observation of the many transsexuals whom I have met who were married at the time they started transitioning and who are now either divorced or becoming divorced as a byproduct of their transition.

So how do you tell your spouse or partner? There is no easy answer to this question. Even if your spouse or partner is aware of your gender identity problem, your history of cross-dressing or your nonconforming gender behavior, the disclosure that you want to change gender will be most likely be both shocking and devastating. No matter what you say after "I want to have gender reassignment surgery." your spouse's life will never be the same again. This is another one of those things that once said, cannot ever be unsaid.

There are so many possible responses from a spouse once you come out to her[11]. "How can you do this to me? "Don't you love me anymore?" "What's going to happen to the kids?" "Get out!" "Why?" "Do you have to do this?" "Can't you just stay a man and be happy living in private as a girl?" "I married a man, I didn't marry a woman." The list of possible responses is potentially endless.

---

[11] I am using female pronouns here for two reasons. One is for readability sake, and the other is because so many transwomen are in heterosexual marriages when they start transitioning. What is stated, though, applies equally to spouses of transmen, or the same-sex partners of both transmen and transwomen.

Your spouse will most likely go through an incredible range of emotions, some of which will continue to be a problem for her for months or years, and which may lead to a desire to separate or divorce. She will feel betrayed because you were always supposed to be there for her. She will feel rejection because she feels you are leaving her and replacing the person she loves with someone (something?) she does not know, nor want. She is going to feel intense sadness because her love is leaving her. Many people say this sadness is very similar to having a life partner die. She is going to feel intense anger because your actions are destroying the marriage. She will feel sorrow for you because she loves you and does not want to see you suffer through a transition. She will be concerned for your children, and both of your extended families. She is going to be embarrassed at having a wife instead of a husband. She may feel responsible for your desire to transition, feeling she somehow forced you to this point. She is going to miss not being able to have sex with you anymore.

Then, she may also be scared, especially if she starts thinking of a divorce and its implications. She will be scared she is going to be spending the rest of her life alone. She will be scared she is going to lose her home. She may start to panic if she does not know where she will be living or how she will survive. She is going to be scared she will not have the financial resources to take care of herself now, or later in life. She is going to be scared her children will grow up with problems because they have a transsexual father who is not present in the household. If she is staying at home raising children, she is going to be scared that no one will be there to help her raise them when she is forced back into the workplace. There are an incredible number of things she may think will happen, and these are but a few.

Now, if you do not think that what will be happening to your spouse emotionally is all that bad, the odds are you are going to feel pretty much the same set of feelings when she says she wants a divorce and wants you out of the house - yesterday.

Have you prepared for the emotional trauma that will arise when you come out to your spouse? Will you have the mental fortitude to continue to transition in the face of a possible divorce? Will your transition stall when your spouse threatens to throw you out if you continue to talk about changing your sex? If you decide that your marriage is more important than transitioning, will your disclosure that you are transsexual permanently damage the relationship you have with your spouse?

Which is worse for you: the emotional pain of going through a divorce, or the emotional pain of not transitioning? Is your love for your spouse great enough for you to sacrifice transitioning and all that transitioning means to you?

Please figure out these issues before you tell your spouse that you want to transition. If you cannot handle the trauma of losing your significant other, then speak with your therapist to find a better way of handling the feelings you are having due to your gender dysphoria. Better yet, just talk with your therapist first. When you and your therapist both feel that transitioning is the only viable treatment for you, and you are mentally strong enough to face and accept the possibility of losing your spouse, family, home, neighbors, etc. as you transition, then you can chance coming out to your spouse.

When you do come out to your spouse or partner, be kind in your words, and give her the support she will need. Answer her questions honestly. Do not lie to her. Do not tell her what you think she wants to hear. Be patient, and understand that the emotions she is going to feel are going to be varied and strong. She will probably emotionally break down, explode angrily, or both. Do not be angry with her in return. Do not threaten her. Be kind and loving not matter what her response. She deserves it.

Give her time to comprehend what you have said. Coming out to a spouse is not a five-minute process. Coming out to someone with whom you are emotionally involved may take days, weeks, months, or even longer in some cases. The things you say, that you think are logical and reasonable, are going to be interpreted by this special someone using an emotion-based thought process. What makes sense to you so clearly is surely not going to make the same kind of sense to her during this major crisis period.

If your spouse wants the two of you to go to a marriage counselor, do not automatically reject the offer. By making that offer, she is saying she hopes there is a resolution that will keep the marriage from disintegrating. Who knows? Maybe the two of you will find a common solution that satisfies the needs of both.

Again, be kind, loving, and supportive no matter how negatively she responds. The burden you are placing on your spouse when you come out is just incredible. Show compassion and love. Remember that you entered into your marriage or committed same-sex union because of your love for your spouse or partner.

PARENTS

Sheer stress and terror were the emotions that constantly ate at me as I prepared to tell my parents I was a transsexual. It did not matter that my parents had found out that I was transgender 28 years earlier when I had a seizure while cross-dressed, and an ambulance took me to the hospital while I was wearing my sister's clothes. I never wanted my parents to discover the full extent of my transgenderism. So even as an adult at the age of forty-four, I was still terrified I would lose the love and respect of my parents should the issue of my being transgender ever be brought to the forefront again.

From a child's point of view, regardless of whether that child is now an adult or not, a parent should always unconditionally love them and be there for them. The child's love for the parents is also supposed to be unconditional. Nevertheless, we are not naïve; issues and beliefs come between parents and children all the time in the real world. What should be the most perfect of relationships, parents and children destroy all the time.

When you prepare to come out to your parents, it is vital that you understand that parents, regardless of their ages, have created expectations in their own minds for their children's lives, and that those expectations are often very much based upon the gender of their children. Therefore, when their daughter discloses that she now wants to be their son, the disclosure destroys all their hopes and dreams of their little girl growing up into a beautiful young woman, a wife, a mother, etc. Even though parents will create an entirely new and wonderful set of expectations for their transitioning child given enough time, for a good while their dreams will be destroyed. Do not doubt for a moment that having their dreams destroyed hurts them; it truly does.

Most children do not realize it, but parents almost invariably have their expectations shattered over an extended period by their children. Children drop out of school. Children switch majors in college to something the parents just cannot understand. A child brings a romantic interest home who has the wrong background, wrong ethnicity, wrong religious beliefs, etc. Four years of college education is thrown away to give guided tours through the wilderness. The list of things children can do to shatter their parents' dreams is simply amazing. However, the key point here is that the expectations are generally shattered one by one over a long period of time.

Because so many of the truly important expectations that parents hold for their children are based upon gender, however, a transitioning child shatters many of his or her parents' dreams at that single moment when he or she states a desire to transition. The parents often feel completely devastated, and the resulting responses of the parents can be truly damaging to the parent / child relationship.

As a parent, I know how hard it is to let your children make their own decisions even when those decisions appear to be destructive. However, many parents simply do not have it within themselves to see their children hurt themselves, regardless of whether the possibility of being hurt is real or just the parent's perception. Often, the parents misinterpret their own shattered expectations as being a truly destructive decision on the part of the child. Add to that strong religious or cultural beliefs, or just a complete misunderstanding of what transgenderism really is, and parents can end up believing that they are going to have to act to save their child from self-destruction.

If their transitioning child is a minor, life for the child can become pure hell with forced therapy, repressive punishments, ejection from the family household, etc. Parents do all of this, though, in the name of love. Even if the transitioning child is an adult, they may abandon their son or daughter until he or she gives up this "nonsensical thought" of changing gender. It almost seems to be a paradox to think that the only way many parents can express their love is to deny their love as a way of forcing their child into compliance. It just makes my brain hurt thinking about it.

So coming out to parents takes a strategy. I took the approach that I would come out to my spouse, my siblings, and a couple of close friends before I told my parents. This way there would be support in place for my parents to help educate them and ease them through the disclosure of my transition. In a way it worked. However, in a way it also backfired.

My wonderful plan backfired in the lingerie department of a Wal-Mart. My 79-year-old mother cornered someone whom I had come out to previously and started asking questions about my well-being. "What's wrong with him? He has lost so much weight. Is he sick? Does he have cancer? Is he gay?" "No, but something close." was the response to the "Is he gay?" question. The "don't ask, don't tell" policy of our family had just gone out the door.

My mother's response was, "Oh. I know what it is." My mother had hoped for my entire adult life that I would overcome my "issues," but apparently I had not, as she had just found out.

As I had planned, my parents immediately had wonderful support from my spouse, sisters, brother, stepsister, and stepbrothers. I, unfortunately, was not yet mentally prepared to talk with my parents about my transsexuality. I was so devastated that I was not able to come out to my parents personally, that I could not even bring myself to talk to them for weeks. When I drove my daughter to college on the day after the Wal-Mart inquisition, I found those 600 miles on the way back home from Savannah to be some of the darkest moments of my life.

After weeks of counseling, I got the courage to talk to my parents. It did not go well, to say the least. When I finally found the strength to call my parent's home, my father answered. I thought this was great as I always saw my father as the one who could adapt to almost any situation, and my mother as being the religious leader of the family. It turned out that my father pretty much ignored everything I had to say on the phone, and started dictating my future attire anytime I planned to visit their home or any of my sibling's homes. I fell apart and hung up on him.

Surprisingly, it was my mother who rescued our relationship three days later. She simply said she had known about me for years and that she was too old to be losing a child she loved so much. I visited my parents shortly after that. Over a three-hour period, I came out to them fully. Since that time, our relationship has vastly improved. Currently, out relationship is excellent.

I learned many lessons from this experience. My parents each had strong beliefs that they were willing to express due to the severity of my problem. My father based his reactions on his love for my mother. My father felt that my coming to their home as a woman would simply devastate my mother, and he was acting to protect her. My mother felt it was way too important to not lose a child. Each of my parents had acted independently and in the best interests of the family as each saw it.

Like the majority of people I came out to, I miscalculated how my parents were going to react to my being transsexual. I had wrongly prejudged my mother, believing religion would be stronger than her love for me. My father, on the other hand, had always maintained an "If I cannot change it, do not worry about it" attitude. I wrongly assumed that this mantra would dictate how he would react to my disclosure of being transsexual.

Like most people of their generation, my parents knew very little about transgenderism or transsexuality, but they were not too old to learn, as I found out. I was able to sit down with my parents and explain to them the feelings I had over the course of my life. I was able to explain the important terms in enough clarity that they could understand how my gender identity was incompatible with my birth sex. They also could comprehend and feel the grief I felt throughout my life because of my gender identity disorder.

I later realized that I had lost control of the coming out process because I allowed too many physical changes to occur before all of the critical people in my life had been informed of my plans to transition. What triggered my mother's 20 questions session was the physical changes that I had been undergoing: weight loss; laser hair removal of my mustache and beard; plucked eyebrows; long hair; pierced ears; long, manicured nails; and new eyeglasses. There were just too many changes that neither I nor anyone else for that matter could adequately explain. How could my parents not possibly ask questions about my health and well-being? They were just trying to be good parents. They are good parents.

Keeping a secret as major as a family member or friend being transsexual is almost impossible. Someone, if pushed, will tell. The bigger the secret, the less pushing it takes. Well, the secret that I was asking my family and friends to hide was enormous, and it did not take much "badgering", as my mother puts it, to drag a secret this big out into the open.

In retrospect, I would suggest that you come out to your parents sooner rather than later. Do not try to hide your transition until that perfect moment. Every day that goes by may be a day when someone slips and gives away your secret. Your parents may be a lot more understanding if they hear about your plans to transition directly from you, in a calm, intelligent manner. It is a lot harder to try to put out a fire than prevent one.

I still think it is a very good idea, though, to have support lined up for your parents before you come out to them if you can arrange it. Maybe this means you come out to an open-minded friend who is also a friend of your parents or a supportive sibling immediately before you make your disclosure to your parents. This will give your parents someone to help them through what will become a very tough time in their lives.

Always be prepared to answer some hard questions when you come out to family members. Many of the questions family members ask will be on issues that you feel are too personal for you to share. This is true especially for parents as parents often think they have the right to know everything about the lives of their children. If you do not want to share something personal with your parents, say for instance something about your sexual relations with your spouse, kindly explain that the issue is personal to you and your spouse, and that you would prefer not to answer their question(s) out of respect for your spouse. Do not be outwardly offensive or belligerent with them. You will only get one chance to come out to your parents, and you should do everything in your power to keep this experience civil. If civility is lost, you may never be able to fully deliver your critical message.

Show your parents the respect they deserve. Give them as much support as you can muster. Give them time to accept you and to build new dreams for you. As much as you expect their love, do not forget to show your love and respect for them in return.

SIBLINGS

Some things in life are simply supposed to be as constant as the laws of physics. Your brother is always your brother, and your sister is always your sister. You must have reached the edge of the universe when your brother wants to become your sister, or your sister wants to become your brother. It is really quite simple; the universe is just broken when you come out to a sibling.

How each of your siblings reacts to your disclosing that you are transitioning is hard to predict. Each of your siblings has a unique relationship with you based on both of your ages, family order, sex, religious beliefs, marital status, etc. Your siblings may also have special relationships with your spouse, your children, and your parents. Disclosing that you are transitioning therefore is not just about you and your siblings; it is also about your siblings' interpretation of how your transition will affect your spouse, children, parents, and their own immediate families as well.

There may be quite an extensive amount of concern expressed by your siblings about your transition, some of which may be very hurtful to you. Siblings feel that because they are family, they are free to be frank and honest with you about their feelings and beliefs, regardless of how misinformed they are. If they do not understand the issues related to an incongruent gender identity, the pain of gender dysphoria, or how you plan to manage your transition, their well-intentioned statements of the facts (as they see them) may be very painful, humiliating, embarrassing, and stigmatizing. Their beliefs may drive a wedge between you and the rest of your family, creating camps that support you and camps that reject you. You may feel ostracized, or you may actually become ostracized.

Siblings have a tendency to believe that they know you inside and out. When you disclose you are transitioning and have hidden a major aspect of your life from them, they can be hurt and feel that your relationship with them has just been a façade. How do they determine which parts of your being are real, and which parts you manufactured to cover up your gender issues? Considering that you say you have had this problem since childhood and have kept it a secret for decades, have you just been lying to them your entire life? Are those joyful memories they had with you something they should forget because somehow, they just were never real?

On the other hand, your siblings may have a very special bond with you, and may be very empathetic towards you. They may support you unconditionally because they love you unconditionally. They may both publicly support you and at the same time express in private their concerns to others. They may base their actions and responses on extremely complex thought processes, or, the most basic of thought processes.

To come out to your siblings, first be prepared to dedicate considerable time to each brother or sister. Arrange with them a time that you can speak to them privately, without interruption from their immediate family or friends. Prepare in advance how you want to present your condition to them. Be prepared to explain how you plan to protect your family and spouse from damage caused by your transition. Try to have an answer for every possible question you think they might ask of you related to family, health, employment, transition concerns, finances, neighbors, friends, etc.

I personally found that each of my siblings had an immediate response that was generally supportive at first. For one, the support only lasted a couple of hours before it turned very sour. For others, the support has been consistently good, although they all have felt sadness and disbelief at times. If you can keep some form of communication open with each sibling, their wounds will heal over time, and their acceptance of the "new" you will grow. For some siblings, however, the time it takes for this acceptance to occur may be much longer than for others. For a few, there may never be enough time.

If you have more than one sibling and you feel you are quickly losing a brother or sister to this issue, seek the assistance of your other brothers and sisters who still support you. Maybe they can help explain to the sibling who is withdrawing from your life how to handle the situation better. They can also bring pressure to bear about keeping the family intact. Every member of the family should have a stake in keeping the family intact, including you.

Do not underestimate the role your parents have in maintaining peace and unity within the family. Your parents most likely do not want to see you hurt, nor do they want to see the family fragmented.

How they express themselves to your siblings can have an incredible impact on whether your family accepts or ostracizes you.

Remember that good relationships require give and take. If your siblings are not comfortable with you, and they do not want you around their children, do not push the issue. Hopefully they will come to understand your transition, and will at some point in time come to support you. When they do, they will be much more open about having you become a part of their immediate families again.

Your siblings may try to project their fears and prejudices upon their kids. They may believe that the sight of the new you will traumatize their children. In reality, their children are probably much more accepting of diverse people then your siblings ever will be. Your siblings will be shocked when you meet their kids the first time, and they realize their children do not really care all that much about your transition.

So be prepared, and be dedicated to winning over your siblings. Friends may come and go, but family is family forever.

CHILDREN

Age, gender, social status, maturity and external influences such as religion or the actions of a spouse/ex-spouse have a very large impact on whether children of transsexuals accept them or not. Because children change so much as they grow, the way your children react to your being transsexual will constantly be in a state of flux until they fully mature.

The main rule of telling your child anything about your transition is to be age appropriate with whatever you disclose to them. A small child is not going to understand a complex explanation of why your gender identity is incongruent with your physical sex. They may not even understand the relationship between genitals and sex. So keep it simple!

At a conference I attended, a daughter of a transwoman gave this wonderful account of how she found out at the age of thirteen from her four-year-old sister that her father was transgender. Her sister, at the wise old age of four simply blurted out while coloring that some people are girls on the inside and girls on the outside, just like she and her sister; but some people are girls on the inside and boys on the outside, just like daddy. So simple, but at the same time, so eloquent. For a young child, there is no need to even try to explain what transsexualism is. The requirement is to explain somehow in very simple terms why it is acceptable that daddy or mommy does not look or act the same as everyone else's daddy or mommy.

Children learn social norms concerning gender very early in life. So if they see you cross-dressed they are immediately going to assume something is wrong. A simple "It's ok for daddy to dress this way." may be all that a small child needs from you to convince them that your actions are appropriate.

If your child is of elementary school age, it is going to be harder. Other kids may taunt your child if they become aware that you are transitioning. The other children are not going to understand your gender issues. Instead, your child's dad being a girl or mom being a boy will most likely be the focus of their taunts. The other kids may simply believe all dads have to be male and all moms must be female.

If you came out early in life to your child and your child sees you as a second mom or second dad, the taunting may start when your child refers to both mommy X and mommy Y. The other children may see any style of family other than the family style that they belong to as being abnormal. The good news is that school systems are far less tolerant of this type of taunting from children or from teachers for that matter, so you may be able to get assistance from the school system to stop any taunting that occurs. It may also be a good idea for your young child to use a nickname for you instead of one of the standard family-oriented names. For instance, try having them substitute Dee-Dee or Mimi for daddy or mommy.

The middle school years are typically the worst years for a child who has a transitioning parent. Unless your child is a truly independent child, there exists an incredible pressure to be accepted. Your child's peers will usually always magnify and exploit every flaw, real or perceived, in your child. Having a transsexual parent can be seen as a huge flaw and as a result have a very negative impact on how your child is accepted. More importantly, having a transsexual parent may strongly influence how your child believes he or she will be accepted. Simply translated, this means they are going to be thinking, "No one is going to like me anymore because of you."

Many children handle this problem by essentially making you vanish as a parent with respect to their friends. They may simply tell their friends that their dad or mom no longer lives with them. If you are divorced and have regular visitation, this presents a problem for them in that they may feel they have to manufacture a story of who the woman or man is they were seen with at such-and-such-a-place. The easiest story for them to tell their friends may be that you are just an aunt or uncle with whom they like spending time.

It may really hurt when your children refer to you as Uncle X or Aunt Y, instead of mom or dad, in the presence of their friends. For you to support your children, though, you are going to have to understand that they feel they have a true need to tell stories like this to their friends. You will also have to understand all the details of the stories they are telling so you can support them if need be. You may not like what is happening or what they say, but you may have to go along with their need to tell these stories until they mature and become independently strong enough to tell their friends the truth about you and their family situation. You cannot correct them for calling you aunt or uncle in front of their friends. You cannot tell one of their friends who calls your home or visits that you are your child's dad or mom unless your child is in agreement with this. You are going to have to support them regardless of how much it hurts you each time.

If your children are high school or college age when you come out to them or they find out about you, their responses can range anywhere from total acceptance to total rejection. A lot of this will depend upon whether they identify with you or feel repulsed by you. Teenagers in particular, often have very negative responses at the thought of having a parent become such an embarrassment to them. If you are a non-custodial parent during the teenage years, all communication with your child may be lost for quite some time. On the other hand, if your child is gender-variant, sexually fluid, or an outcast at school, they may relate their own pains of rejections to your experience, and be more readily accepting of you in the process.

The general feeling of those who have gone through a total loss of communication with their children is to never let your children think that you do not continue to love them, or think that they are unwanted in your life. Although children may reject the attempts that you make to communicate with them during their teenage years, as they mature, they may come to understand the complexities of gender dysphoria and the reasons behind your transition. If and when they reach this point, hopefully the years of letters, birthday presents and emails you sent to them without a response will let them realize that you wish to restore relations with them when they are ready.

In addition, a scorned ex-spouse can do incredible damage to your relationships with your children, especially if you do not have physical custody of them. Always show your children that you love them and care about their well-being. This is the only defense you have against an ex-spouse that constantly belittles you. Your kids can independently reason. If they constantly see love and affection from you, they will eventually reason your ex-spouse is wrong about you. Do not try to explain to your children why your ex-spouse is wrong about you. It may make the children defensive about the ex-spouse, and actually validate the claims your ex makes about you. The contempt you show for your ex-spouse may very well overwhelm the love you show your children, so do not show any contempt or anger towards your ex in the presence of your children. Love and care for your children. It is the only cure for the damage done by a scorned ex.

Do not abandon your children because you think coming out to them will ruin or has ruined their lives. **You have an obligation to raise your children to adulthood regardless of whatever hardships you face during your gender transition.** If you really want to ruin their lives, abandon them. Nothing hurts a child more than rejection from a parent, even a transsexual parent. If you truly believe your child will not be able to accept you undergoing a transition and will disown you as his or her parent, then you should spend some serious time contemplating whether transitioning at this point in your life is appropriate. **Maybe delaying your transition five or ten years, as much as that may hurt you, is the best gift you can ever give to your family.**

I truly hope that your relationships with your children survive your transition.

FRIENDS AND NEIGHBORS

A friendship can be fleeting, or a friendship can last a lifetime. I like to think that friends can be broken down into two major categories: acquaintances, and true friends. Acquaintances come and go in your life. When they go, you may feel a loss or you may feel nothing at all. Nevertheless, acquaintances do go away, and new acquaintances fill their spots in your life.

A true friend is generally your friend through thick or thin. Correspondingly, you are also their true friend through thick or thin. Years may go by sometimes between visits with a true friend, but your friendship always picks up where it last left off. True friends are timeless.

Most people have very few true friends. Many people confuse very good acquaintances with true friends. There are really good acquaintances to whom you may trust to tell everything, but will these good friends be there for you after they meet and fall in love with some new girl or guy? If their job transfers them to some far away location, will you ever hear from them beyond the first month? Will you travel across the country to share a birthday or Christmas with them once they move on? Can you call them, years after they have moved away, to ask their advice on a personal problem?

I hope you see the differences between acquaintances and true friends, because you must treat a true friend as a family member when you come out. In many ways, a true friend is like a brother or sister. When you have known true friends for years or decades, coming out is either going to be a shock, or something that they have been long expecting. They may be taken aback when you first say you are transsexual, but you may be very surprised at their overall level of acceptance. A true friend, who has been your friend for most of your life, is going to see things in you that other people may have overlooked. They will have been there to support you through the happy moments of your life and those points when you reached rock bottom. They will have built up a tolerance to your flaws that allows them to stick with you through those really awful times in your life.

Coming out to a true friend requires the same level of thought, disclosure, and effort as coming out to a family member. However, a positive response to your disclosure may be far quicker in coming, and may also be more affirmative than the responses you receive from family members. I believe there are two reasons for this. The first and most important reason is that you were there for your true friends at all those critical points in their lives, just as they were in yours. So, being a true friend to someone carries with it an elevated level of respect. The more respect you have from someone, the easier it is for them to accept you. The second reason is that relationships between true friends often break or bend gender boundaries anyway. An alternate way of stating this is that two true friends are often emotionally bound to one another beyond the limits of what gender norms or societal limits normally allow between "regular" friends.

Several times I have heard that true friends are often more upset over not being trusted with the transsexual secret than they were with the fact their best friend is transsexual. Although it is going to take time for a true friend to adapt to you in your new gender, there is really a great chance that they will still be there for you when the dust settles. This is not a guarantee, however. True friends can be transphobic, religious extremists, or bigots, just like anyone else. I just hope that the people whom you have made your closest friends are nothing like that though.

On the other hand, you need to treat acquaintances, figuratively, like children. You need to tell them only what is appropriate for them. Not every single acquaintance in your life has to know your entire history. What you need to tell each acquaintance is going to be highly influenced by your own opinions of each person.

The amount of information you disclose is therefore going to have to be proportional to the level of empathy, understanding, and support that you wish to create in each person. As I mentioned earlier, I personally took the approach that I would answer anyone's questions as long as it did not require me to disclose confidential information entrusted to me by someone else, such as my spouse.

I feel very strongly that unfettered honesty about the hardships of being transsexual and transitioning has an enormous impact on the level of respect your acquaintances will have for you. Someone who respects you for having survived and overcome a lifelong emotional struggle may support you even if he or she does not agree with the concept of people being transsexual, or with people transitioning from one sex to another.

No matter how much effort you put into coming out to a friend, be it an acquaintance or true friend, you still may lose them as a friend. Your gender and your friend's gender are both integral parts of your relationship. Each of your genders implies certain limits on the physical contact, subject matter in conversations, and conduct permitted within your relationship. Gender also affects how your friends interpret your actions and the stories you tell. Society allows men to get away with certain things and women with others.

Changing your gender therefore can contribute to the breakup of a friendship even though your friend accepted you when you first came out. For instance, will your single male friend still want to talk with you about the girls he scored with as you become a girl? Will that guy who has a flirtatious relationship with you still be interested in being your friend as you become a boy? If you start hanging out in a book club with other women, will your drinking buddies still want you as their pal, especially if the other women in the book club are their wives?

Gender has such a big influence in our lives, especially with friends. Often it is harder to maintain an existing relationship after you come out than it is to just come out.

Transitioning allows you to express parts of yourself that you have most likely kept hidden from public view, and I do not mean just your flair for dressing. You will get the chance to do things that you have always wanted to do, but refrained from doing in the past, because you felt doing so might just have given away your little transsexual secret. This freedom to be yourself will cause you to change in very subtle ways, in addition to the obvious physical changes that transitioning entails. One of the subtle changes may very well be the thing that a friend does not want to accept.

Is this fair? Of course it is. You decided which people were your friends by evaluating their individual attributes, behaviors, beliefs, actions, and deeds. Then you evaluated how all their characteristics combined made you feel. Your friends also went through this process when they decided to accept you as their friend. Your newfound freedom of expression or interests, however, may now be a turn off for them. If some of your friends turn their backs on you because of these minor things, does that mean they dislike transsexuals? No, it just means you are no longer the person you used to be, and they do not find the characteristics of the new you appealing.

On the flip side of this, when you transition, your friends may expect you to change and pick up certain attributes of the gender you are transitioning to. If you do not pick up these attributes, and you retain too many attributes of your prior gender, not necessarily meaning your physical attributes, they may also reject you. For instance, maybe they find your behavior while attending sporting events a bit too crude for a woman. Maybe they feel you express fears, worries, or opinions during or after transitioning that are more "appropriate" for your old gender.

If you convince your friends to accept you in a new gender, they are going to expect you to meet their expectations for that gender. If you are a transwoman and your friend likes girls that are rough and adventuresome, your becoming an ultra-feminine woman may just turn your friend off, especially if he truly accepts you as a woman. For a transman, maybe the "new" you is a bit too masculine and aggressive for some of your friends to accept.

Hopefully your true friends will be more tolerant of the changes that occur as you transition, thereby providing both of you the time needed to mature a bit in your new relationship. Acquaintances come and go though, and you may just lose a couple on this trail you are blazing.

COWORKERS / COMING OUT ON THE JOB

What do you create when you take a diverse group of people, with little commonality in beliefs, morals, openness and tolerance, and stick them in a small confined space where many of them do not want to be in the first place? A workplace.

Coming out on the job is just about the one thing no one really wants to do. Coming out on the job brings with it the very real prospect that you may lose your job and the risk that you may be unable to find subsequent employment in the area where you live. I hate to be overly negative, but if you come out as transsexual at work, you may lose your job irrespective of the laws of your state or country, or the diversity policy of your employer.

As of the start of 2009, only 13 of the 50 states in the U.S. had anti-discrimination statutes that protected gender identity or gender expression in the workplace. There was no law at the national level within the U.S. that offered employment protections to transgender workers. And only 30% percent of Fortune 500 companies protected their transgender employees explicitly in their diversity statements. Being a transgender employee, therefore, was a very risky proposition at best. Depending how much has changed since this book was written, being a transgender employee may still be a very risky proposition.

Success in coming out at work is measured in several ways. The most obvious measure of success is your ability to retain your job. If you do manage to keep your job after you come out in the workplace, will promotions occur over time, or will management overlook you for advancement forever? At review time, will your evaluations be fair? Will the assessment of your work assignments be without bias? Will the workplace become so hostile that you feel your only option is to quit? Workplace discrimination comes in many shapes and flavors, all of which are very ugly and distasteful.

In addition to the risks associated with coming out as transgender at work, gender inequalities in the workplace may very likely expose a transwoman to the same biases that negatively affect genetic women's authority, pay and advancement opportunities. I have heard many genetic women question why transwomen would ever want to become women considering the gender biases women face at work and in life in general.

At the risk of sounding arrogant, many people are really stupid and stubborn when it comes to their jobs, and as a result, they experience extreme grief when they begin their transitions. If you recognize before you start your transition that your boss is a bigot, and he openly expresses hate towards gays and transsexuals, it may be best to find a new job before you transition. If you have seen other gay, lesbian or gender non-conforming employees suffer harassment by coworkers, be demoted, or be let go, get a safer / better job before you come out. Do not wait until a very bad situation develops before you start searching for alternate employment.

A lot of transwomen lose both upper body strength and muscle mass as they transition. Many transmen do not develop as much height, body mass and strength as their genetically male brothers. If you will not physically be able to do your job after transitioning, seek occupational retraining and switch professions before you transition.

If you work in a field of employment that typically employees people of one specific gender (e.g. mechanic, construction worker, cosmetic sales representative, etc.) prior to transitioning, you may be forced to switch your job in the future as the result of your transition. If you believe that you do not have the skill set to do a gender-neutral job or a job that is dominated by people of the gender you are switching to, then I would recommend that you get the education and training that will allow you to perform a job in your new gender before you transition. If possible, switch to that new job before you come out at work.

Are you mentally prepared to do the same job you are currently doing in a different gender? For instance, a woman can certainly be an electrician, and an excellent electrician at that. However, if you are currently an electrician and you transition from male to female, will you still have the desire to be an electrician after your gender switch? Do not just think someone else's prejudices may be the reason you have to find a new job. Your own prejudices may make you uncomfortable enough that you may wish to leave your job voluntarily.

Do not be foolish and think you are so valuable an employee that your employer will not fire you because you are irreplaceable. An employer can replace almost every employee. If your employer can find a replacement for you should you quit, become disabled, or die, then he will be able to find a replacement for you should he decide to let you go because he does not like the fact you are transsexual.

Keep in mind that it is always easier to find a job while you have a job than when you are unemployed. When you apply for a job while you are employed, you have an implied worth as your current employer must think well enough of you to be paying you for the work that you do. Having current employment gives you bargaining power as you do not appear desperate for work, you still have an income to support yourself, and you can turn down any offer that you believe is unfair.

If your employer lets you go because you came out as being transsexual, you will have certain negative biases applied to you when you apply for a new job no matter how many positive referrals you bring to the interview simply because you are currently unemployed. For many employers, the fact that you do not currently have a job means you did not do your last job well enough for your employer to retain you, even if you left voluntarily. If you are lucky enough to receive a job offer while unemployed, being unemployed considerably reduces your ability to negotiate for better salary and benefits.

Before you come out at work and before you start to transition, please take time to consider the combined effects of loss of employment and being single. Even if you are married when you start to transition, there is a high probability that transitioning may lead to a separation or divorce. If you end up becoming single due to your transition, or are currently single, how will you survive if you lose your job and cannot find a new job in the midst of your transition? Will you lose your home or apartment when you cannot pay the mortgage or the rent? Will the finance company repossess your car when you cannot make the payments? How will you find a job if you are homeless and have no transportation in addition to being transsexual? This is not a pretty scenario and it can become an ugly reality very, very quickly.

You can have a very large influence over how smoothly your coming out at work goes. Some of the things you may be required to do to remain employable, for instance obtaining a college degree or undergoing occupational training, may take years to complete. Start making the changes you need to make to maintain employability early, and be willing to make some sacrifices along the way. In other words, do not let the four weeks of vacation or some other great benefit that you are getting from your current employer prevent you from switching jobs, if that is what is needed to remain employed throughout your transition.

The most important thing you can do to ensure a smooth transition at work is to choose an employer that will both accept and protect a transitioning employee. Many large corporations have diversity policies that either include explicit protections for gender identity and gender expression, or have catchall clauses in their diversity policies that provide protections to any person capable of doing his or her job properly. Diverse people bring ingenuity to the workplace, and some corporations value that. A company that implements a diversity policy to recruit and retain its workforce is going to be active in making sure its employees follow the diversity policy closely. This is important to note, because a diversity policy that is not enforced is useless.

If you cannot get employment in a large corporation, there are plenty of small businesses with open-minded or diverse owners. Finding transgender-friendly small businesses may be hard to do especially in conservative regions. I would recommend networking with others at support groups to help identify potential employers.

If you do not live in a state or municipality that has an anti-discrimination statute that protects gender identity in the workplace, consider moving somewhere with better transgender protections before you start to transition. Because gender identity discrimination in hiring is so difficult to prove, be aware that moving to a new state or municipality in the midst of your transition may not offer you much protection, even when anti-discrimination statutes are on the books in your new place of residence.

If you do relocate somewhere that offers employment protections, find employment and get a history of positive reviews (always get your reviews in writing!) before you make your transition public. If you find yourself being discriminated against at your new job after you come out in the workplace, you will have a much better chance of retaining your job or winning a claim in court if you can show a history of positive reviews and evaluations prior to coming out, followed by sudden prejudicial actions after you came out. Not very many people who are transitioning wish to end up in court, but you will need to be able to produce hard evidence that shows that your boss discriminated against you should you be forced into filing a discrimination complaint or suit.

Coming out in the workplace is going to be much different than coming out to friends or family. While some of your coworkers may be your friends (as in acquaintances), many will just be people who associate with you solely because you work for the same employer. They are there. You are there. You are forced to interact together. It is that simple. Some of your coworkers may see you as a friend, a resource, or a fun person. Others may view you as a jerk, an impediment to their success, or a nuisance. They may hold prejudicial feelings about you even before you come out, even if they have had little or no experience directly dealing with you.

Plan carefully how you want to come out at work. Try to determine which people you must talk with, and in what order. You may initially just need to come out to your immediate boss and possibly someone in human resources. If you are working for a small company, it may be the owner, general manager, or both.

You do not want to come out to coworkers before coming out to management. Telling someone that you are transsexual and expecting him or her to keep it a secret at work is just being naïve. Take it from someone who was naïve and got "outed" at work by a coworker.

What you need to tell your management is going to vary case-by-case. Your personal relationship with your supervisor and the size of the employer will greatly influence the amount of personal information you will feel obligated to share.

For example, I sub-contract to a small consulting firm that in turn contracts to a major government contractor. My relationship with the owners of the small consulting management company is very close and personal. This closeness allowed me to take the three owners to dinner one evening, giving me the opportunity to explain to them that I was preparing to go full-time as a woman. I shared many personal details over dinner, and all three owners became supportive of me. They agreed to keep my transition private until I was ready to disclose my transition plans to the larger corporation.

However, I made a mistake one night on a phone call with a coworker from the larger company, and I ended up coming out to him. About two weeks later, he let it slip to someone else on the staff that I was transsexual. Soon everyone on the staff started asking questions and talking about my being transsexual. This is not what I wanted to happen, as my transition was becoming disruptive to the workplace. I knew that this situation, and the disruption it was causing, could easily become the justification needed to terminate my contracts.

As soon as I found out about of the rumors, I got in touch with the division manager of the larger corporation and told her I was transitioning. Because this corporation has such a strong diversity policy, she handled my disclosure very professionally and did not require much personal information. To her, this was just a work issue that the diversity policy covered, and she would address it as such. Management notified my coworkers of my transition and my name change, and instructed them to treat me as a woman without prejudice according to the established diversity policy. Life suddenly was very good. I feel I am incredibly lucky in this regard.

To my advantage, I was working at home about 95% of the time when the disclosure at work occurred. Do not underestimate how much of a benefit working from home can be to a person in transition. Telecommuting gave me the opportunity to get many of the prerequisite tasks that are required to go full-time out of the way before the first day I walked into the corporate office presenting as a woman. I was even able to have jaw surgery done to make my jaw more feminine before the first time I had to meet my coworkers. If you can find a job that lets you work at home while you prepare to go full-time, take it!

Once you disclose that you are transitioning to management, you cannot let your transition affect your job performance or someone else's job performance. This means you must not talk about your transition at work, or let it interfere with productivity or operations in any way. If coworkers want to talk with you about your transition, and you wish to share your story with them, talk with them at an official break, over lunch, or have them contact you by phone after work. Just keep in mind that office gossip can kill your career. What you entrust to one coworker today, may be office fodder tomorrow.

Coworkers, both managers and peers, are going to be more willing to accept you if you have their respect as a person, and if they respect the work you do for the company before you announce your transition. If they like you and you have a good relationship with them before you come out, you are likely to fare better.

Your coworkers may have some real problems accepting you in the workplace regardless of the diversity policy or laws that are in effect. Some may have strong religious beliefs. Some may be offended when you use "their" bathroom. Your coworkers may be curious or confused about your status. They might not feel comfortable talking with you about work issues, and they may feel very uncomfortable talking to you regarding transition issues. As noted earlier, gender changes significantly alter the way you communicate with others. Do not assume that everyone you work with is going to want to talk with you about your transition.

If you are in a management position yourself, transitioning may force you to learn a new management style to match your new gender. Subordinates will label a transwoman who barks orders like a man a bitch. Conversely, they will consider a transman who meekly manages to be a wimp or pushover. A transwoman is going to have to learn the nuances of managing as a woman, and a transman is going to have to learn the nuances of managing as a man. If you do not show the management traits appropriate for your new gender, you will lose the respect of both your subordinates and your own management.

A major factor in retaining your job is going to be whether your transition is perceived to, or actually hurts the company's image, the company's income, or the productivity of your department or division. There is a fine line between legitimate business need and discrimination sometimes. For instance, let us say you are in a sales position. It is early in your transition and you do not present well. A fair number of your existing customers are switching to other vendors because they are not comfortable dealing with you, and as a result, you are not meeting your sales quota. Is it discrimination when your boss temporarily removes you from the sales position, or fires you because the loss of revenue is jeopardizing the company's profitability? Would a judge see his action as a form of discrimination, or a reasonable business decision based upon your poor performance? Would you prevail if you filed suit against your employer? Would a reasonable jury expect you to have found a way to retain the customers that you lost as you transitioned?

If you are lucky enough to survive coming out to your management and coworkers, you may experience a backlash from your employer's customers. When you think about the term customers, you must do it with a broad mind. If a corporation employs you, your customers may be the public, other businesses or the government. If you work for the government, your customers may be the taxpayers or corporations. If you work for a school system, your customers may be students or parents.

Customers can be rude, obnoxious, and very damaging to your career. They are detached from you on almost every level. They may not care at all that you are transgender, or they may respond very prejudicially because you are. The problem with customers is that there is very little that you can do to control them in most instances. If your customers are students, parents, the public, or taxpayers, they are free to express whatever biases and prejudices they hold, and your employer may be unable to do anything to suppress their outrage and ignorance.

If you are an educator, your employment may be at great risk as teachers in particular are specifically prone to fervent and public attacks by parents who wrongly believe that transsexuals are sexual predators, immoral, or bad influences upon their children. Often, parents will carry out these character attacks at school board meetings, making the story of your transition public. News organizations, both local and national, may pick up the story of your transition and the efforts being made to oust you. Prompt legal action may be required to force the school system to not reassign you or terminate your employment.

If you are employed by a religious organization, you may have no legal rights or remedies should a backlash occur either by parents or by the religious organization itself. Many state laws and the most recently proposed national anti-discrimination legislation provide exemptions for religious organizations. Legislators allow sexual orientation and gender identity discrimination to occur in certain cases so that religious organizations can follow their religious tenets without interference from the government. Unfortunately, freedom of religion considerations generally triumph over employment discrimination in many jurisdictions.

The exemption for religious organizations brings up an interesting point. Each state or municipality may have a certain number of exemptions in its discrimination statutes. You really have to take time to research which state and municipal laws will protect you should you be discriminated against, and you must read all of the small print. In addition to religious organization exemptions, small businesses with less than 10 or 15 employees are also often exempt from discrimination statutes in many jurisdictions.

Coming out to coworkers and retaining your job requires a lot of insight, research, planning and execution in order to be successful. Although you might survive just walking in one day and declaring you are now a man or a woman, you just might not.

Sometimes the best solution to the problem of coming out at work is not the most obvious. I met a transwoman who instead of relocating or finding a new job pressed her company to change its diversity policy so that it included gender identity and gender expression protections. She apparently was very coy about this, and got these changes through under the premise that other companies in the same employment sector were enacting this type of diversity policy change to attract better and more diverse employees. The company had no idea she was a transwoman in waiting. Shortly after the company approved the new diversity policy, she came out to her management and coworkers. She still has her job, and it is a very good job at that.

Even though many people lose their jobs when they come out at work, more and more are able to keep and successfully perform their existing jobs in their new gender. Having survived the gay and lesbian workplace movement, many companies are now accepting of transgender employees and treat them well. Each year, the number of employers that are adding gender identity and gender expression to their diversity policies is ever increasing. Many states are updating their laws in a similar fashion, and many state governments have implemented executive orders to prevent gender discrimination in state jobs.

When the fears and anxieties of coming out at work are bearing down on you, try to relax and do all that is required to complete your transition. I have found that the fear of coming out at work is one of the most common reasons that people stall in their transitions. Be smart, and plan carefully as to when, where, how and to whom you will come out to in the workplace. Then, follow your plan when the time is right.

The shock of having a transsexual coworker eventually wears off, and life in due course returns to normal in the workplace in many cases. Just keep in mind that not all employers implement or enforce an inclusive diversity policy. In some cases, transgender employees simply cannot overcome the employment discrimination that exists in a particular workplace. If you find yourself in a bad employment situation, move on to a new job before your employment history becomes tarnished, or something worse befalls you.

STRANGERS

There is no way to appear entirely like a genetic woman or man overnight, if ever. Transitioning is a journey that takes years. No matter how hard you try, someone might figure out that you are transsexual along the way. Just because some people figure out that your face is too masculine for a woman or your frame is too frail for a man, does not entitle them to stare, talk about you, or harass you.

People you do not know do not have a right to know all about you. What you tell them about your being transsexual, if you tell them anything at all, is entirely your own choice. The exception to this rule is when the information being solicited is directly related to medical, legal or otherwise critical situations.

I have found that just initiating a conversation with a stranger is the most important tool that you can use to fight a stranger's immediate negative response to your presence. Generally, what you talk to them about is completely irrelevant. What is important is that you get them to interact with you by initiating a conversation with them.

Many strangers who detect that you are transitioning are going to categorize you as a cross-dresser, transvestite, transgender, transsexual, or some type of sexual pervert depending upon their knowledge or lack thereof of gender issues. They will then assign to you the value or lack of value that they hold for that class of person. Essentially, they classify and treat you as an object that has assigned to it a specific value, often a sub-human value.

When you hold conversations with strangers who have done this objectification of you, you force them to re-evaluate you as a person. This re-evaluation assigns you a more precise value as they are forced to get a sense of who you are through your words, expressions, and mannerisms whether they want to or not. In essence, initiating a conversation forces them to reclassify and treat you as a person, not an object.

The change in attitude that occurs in some people is almost instantaneous. Even though they do not have a clue as to why you are dressed as a woman or a man, they immediately reclassify you as a person. It is truly amazing how quickly you can force a positive response in someone by simply talking with him or her.

Do not believe, though, that you can manage all strangers this way. A small subset of individuals whose prejudices are so great feel they are justified in assaulting, crippling, or murdering transsexuals. Studies have shown that the murder rate for transsexuals is considerably higher per capita than just about any other minority group in America. Be smart, and be careful about whom you attempt to befriend.

If you are transitioning from male to female, you are especially at risk. You run a higher of risk being sexually assaulted or having other crimes committed against you, because in addition to the risks associated with you being transsexual, aggressors may see you as being female and vulnerable. Being seen as a potential victim is just a risk that comes with being a woman in Western society. Being transsexual just adds to this risk, so always be cautious.

You will find that there are some strangers who have a legitimate need to know some parts of your transition story. Health care professionals are one such group. If you are a political activist, you may want to disclose parts of your story to gain support for your cause. What you disclose to a stranger, however, should be limited to what you feel is required and you should always understand that it is your personal information that your disclosure is making public. Hence, your disclosure should be limited to the information you feel is appropriate and with which you are completely comfortable disclosing. Just because a stranger asks you a personal question does not mean you are obligated to answer it.

HIDING IN PLAIN SIGHT

In order to qualify for gender reassignment surgery, the World Professional Association for Transgender Health (WPATH[12]) *Standards of Care* require that you adopt a new or evolving gender role or gender presentation in everyday life for at least one full year. Transsexuals know this as the Real-Life Experience. The goals of this requirement are to make sure you have an understanding that changing your sex will have immediate, profound personal and social consequences, and to make sure you have an awareness of the familial, vocational, interpersonal, educational, economic, and legal consequences that will result as you transition.

In more simple terms, this requirement simply states that at some point in time you are going to have to venture out of your home as your new self and face the world in every aspect of your life if you want to continue on the path towards gender reassignment surgery. You may be ready to take this major step, but the world may not be quite so willing to accept the new you with wide-open arms. It is not that everyone in the world dislikes transsexual people, even though it may seem that way sometimes; it is just that the majority of people do not handle gender confusion very well. They wrongly expect human gender to be binary, i.e. male or female, and immutable.

Each person has a number of gender cues that everyone around him or her immediately recognizes. These include physical characteristics such as hair length and style; facial structure; voice; laryngeal prominence; neck length and girth; breast size; ratio of the sizes of the chest, waist and hips; leg length and shape; feet and hand size; body

---

[12] http://www.wpath.org

hair; location of body fat, etc. The face in particular has many secondary sex characteristics that will be discussed later.

The body as a whole also gives off cues about gender, both while in motion and while at rest. Simply put, women walk, run, sit and stand differently than men. Particular motions, for instance how a hand moves during a conversation, may also relay a sense of femininity or masculinity.

The voice has a number of audible characteristics that people consider male or female. There is pitch, resonance, intonation, circumflexion, melody, etc. People consider sentences that are choppy and without many pitch variations as being masculine, while they consider flowing and musical sentences to be feminine, regardless of pitch.

When another person encounters you, that person's brain unconsciously recognizes all of your visible and audible gender cues. The brain immediately classifies each gender cue as being either male or female. In a perfect world, all of your gender cues would be entirely of one gender, but as you transition this is often not the case. If you present both female and male gender cues, the other person's brain may not automatically be able to determine your physical gender, and he or she may need to make a more conscious determination of your gender.

If you appear androgynous or you are not convincingly male or female in your presentation, you may trigger uneasiness in the people you encounter, and you may find yourself subjected to whatever prejudices these people hold. You may find yourself ignored, stared at, harassed, refused service, verbally abused, assaulted, or in some other way discriminated against.

Therefore, to live full-time as a transwoman or transman, you are going to have to convincingly present yourself so that you may pass freely in society as a woman or man without prejudice. You will additionally have to learn to fit in, displaying behavior that is appropriate for the gender role you are adapting.

The net result is that after you finally come out to your world, you essentially work yourself back into the closet. This seems a bit counter intuitive. The best I can explain it is that when you initially come out you are announcing to everyone in your world that you are transsexual and that you are about to undertake a huge, life altering change. Then as you start the physical transformation phase of your transition, the physical changes that you undergo make you appear more and more like a member of your identified gender. When you reach a certain level of physical change, such as that which results from having undergone facial feminization surgery or years of testosterone therapy, there may come a time that the majority of people end up just seeing you as a genetic woman or man unless you tell them otherwise.

If this happens to you, you will almost certainly feel a pressure to preserve the image people form of you. If they cannot tell you transitioned, why should you tell them? Therefore, it becomes your choice whom you inform that you are transsexual and whom you let believe you are just an ordinary woman or man just like everyone else. To those that you do not tell, you hide your past, and suddenly you find that you are back in the closet again.

What a tough game we play.

PASSING

Society can be very unforgiving with its binary expectations of gender. When you walk out the front door of your home each day you need the people you encounter to see you as a woman or a man, not as a man dressed like a woman, or a woman trying to appear as a man.

The term "passing" refers to the act of presenting yourself in public in your identified gender, so that others perceive you as being a genetic woman or man. Simply put, you look just as normal or abnormal as any other girl or guy on the street. The two underlying goals of passing are not to be read[13] as a transsexual, and to have others assess you to be a member of the gender to which you are transitioning. Therefore, to pass successfully requires that you alter or suppress enough of your birth gender cues such that the people that you encounter no longer judge you as being of your birth gender.

Some steps taken by transwomen to alter their natural gender cues include taking female hormones and testosterone suppressors, having facial feminization surgery, augmenting their breasts, and removing their facial, body, leg and arm hair. Other less drastic actions include manicures and pedicures, makeup, wearing undergarments that restrict the waist or enhance the bust line, and wearing wigs or hair extensions.

Transmen who desire to pass successfully have a significant number of gender cues altered by just taking the hormone testosterone, commonly referred to as "T", which causes male secondary sex characteristics to develop in the face, causes the growth of facial hair, increases muscle mass, deepens the voice and triggers the growth of body, leg and arm hair. Hormone therapy may reduce breast size in some, but transmen often resort to either binding their breasts or surgically removing their breasts to have a more masculine torso.

For transmen and transwomen alike, having gender appropriate hairstyles and clothing is a necessity. During the early stages of transitioning, many transsexuals wear what they believe is appropriate clothing but often it is not. For instance, the majority of genetic women dress casually at the grocery store, the mall and even restaurants. Transwomen in the early stages of transitioning, however, will often overdress by wearing skirts, dresses and high heels while the genetic women around them are wearing jeans and flats. Transmen are often no better, having that kind of yuppie in a sweater and khakis look when

---

[13] Being read is when others see you as being a member of your birth gender and not a member of the gender in which you identify.

the genetic guys around them are wearing ill-fitting jeans and old tee shirts.

Dressing successfully thus requires that you pay attention to the people around you and that you wear items that are appropriate for your age, the event you are going to, the time of day, season of the year, weather, etc. Simply put, you have to wear what makes sense and what is appropriate. You cannot just dress according to the image of femininity or masculinity that you maintain in your head.

This can be a very hard lesson to learn. If you are a transwomen, your life long desire to wear mini-skirts does not give you carte blanche to wear one wherever you wish after you start to transition. This rule applies even if you have great legs, mini-skirts absolutely flatter you, and you feel you have the God given right to dress as you please.

If you are going to a dance club in which everyone is similarly dressed, then a mini-skirt may be situationally appropriate. However, in another social setting just how much unwanted attention are you going to garner by wearing a mini-skirt rather than just dressing a bit more casually and appropriately? Although it may be positive attention that you seek, it only takes one person in a crowd, a store or a bar who focuses on you because your attire caught his eye to resultantly read you as being a transsexual and to cause an adverse situation to develop.

Regardless of the depth of your wardrobe, dressing alone is not going to make you pass successfully. You are going to have to alter enough gender cues that others do not automatically read you as a member of your birth gender. You may not realize how many gender cues you give off, or how many of these conflict with your identified gender.

Basically, if you feel that people are reading you everywhere you go, you need to stop and figure out which gender cues are giving you away. Ask a friend whom you trust to give you her honest opinion, and do not argue with her if she truly tells you how she feels! If she tells you have bad posture or walk like a cowboy, it is probably true. Listen to her and then try to correct whatever gender cues you project that are

inappropriate for your new gender. Afterwards, if people are still
reading you, keep asking other people you trust the same question until
you determine everything about yourself that gives you away and you
figure out a way to correct all the gender cues that you can correct.

No matter how hard you try though, you may never change all of
your birth gender cues. Surgical solutions such as facial feminization
surgery may just not be realistically obtainable for everyone. Some
gender cues cannot be erased by any surgical procedures or by dress.
For instance, you cannot become un-tall or alter the size of your hips.
You can, however, wear clothing that flatters your body build, and you
can learn how to counter inquiries into physical characteristics that are
atypical for your identified gender. When I get asked about my height
(6' 1") by men, I often respond flirtatiously "Look, you either like tall or
you don't like tall; Which is it (with a devilish smile)?" This
immediately tells the person commenting about my height that I am
confident about my height. You would be surprised how many men
suddenly like very tall women and stop making comments about my
height when I tell them this.

Regardless of the techniques you may employ to pass, being a
transsexual and living full-time requires that you accept that from time
to time people will read you no matter what you do. Some people are
just more sensitive than others in detecting and classifying gender cues.
Nevertheless, do not let this disappoint you. Yes, it is true that not
being read makes life easier, but it is also true that having people never
read you at all is not a requirement to transition. There is an old adage,
"You can fool some of the people all of the time, and all of the people
some of the time, but you cannot fool all of the people all of the time."
People who try to live their lives in complete stealth eventually end up
being read and outed.

The moral here is to realize that doing as much as you can to pass
can make your everyday life much better, but do not ever believe you
will never be read. If you ever reach the point where you pass so well
that you almost never get read, you then pick up the responsibility of
determining which of the people with whom you associate really need

to know of your past. Living in complete stealth places an extreme burden on those whom you expect to hold secret your history. Do you really want to pass so well that you end up living your life in fear of being outed?

Living in complete stealth also carries with it great risks. Will someone misinterpret your passing too well as being intentionally deceptive at a critical moment of your life? Will someone whom you know react hurtfully or violently if you are outed to them at the wrong time?

As farfetched as it seems, being outed while living in stealth may result in extreme violence against you, and possibly your death. For example, if you are a post-op transwoman and you have sexual relations with a heterosexual guy who does not know your past, what reaction will he have if one of his buddies sends him a text message that says you were once a guy while you are lying together in bed immediately after intercourse? Is he an understanding soul? Or deep down inside, is he a closet transphobe? Will his reaction be calm or brutally violent? It is vital to remember that your personal safety must always take precedence over passing and stealth regardless of how badly you want to be just another girl or guy.

Moreover, as important as passing may seem to you, there is an argument suggesting transwomen and transmen should just be proud of whom they are, and that they should not try to mold themselves to fit the binary gender expectations of society. In theory, this argument has a lot of merit as people should be free to live and act as they feel without trying to live up to society's binary gender expectations. As noble as that argument is, swimming against the tide is terribly hard. Much social engineering is going to have to occur before society matures to the point of having no gender-based expectations of how people present themselves. Until this societal change occurs, your ability to pass will directly influence other people's reactions to your presence. I do not know about the rest of you, but I do not want to wait for society to change before I can live a relatively normal life again.

FITTING IN

When you work to make yourself pass as a man or woman, in essence, you are changing your physical gender cues to influence the gender attribution that occurs when other people meet you for the first time. One gender cue not yet discussed and which others do not usually attribute during that first glimpse is the gender appropriateness of your behavior.

Even though we may think or dream of ourselves in our identified gender throughout our lives, until we start to transition the people around us see and treat us as members of the gender to which we were born. With each passing day, with each and every experience, family, friends, and society teach us the proper way to handle all of life's little situations according to the gender-based rules of behavior.

Some people do not choose to follow the gender rules of society completely, but almost everyone follows some or all of the gender rules expected of them to some extent no matter how rebellious they are. Those who step outside the bounds of these rules often are criticized, ridiculed, or ostracized. Schools are notorious for the peer pressure placed upon students by other students to follow gender appropriate behavior.

The girls and guys around you have the gender specific social skills they possess because everyone in their lives treated them as girls or guys from the start. You are going to begin living as a woman or man somewhere in the middle of your life with no manual that covers the gender-specific life lessons that you missed during that first segment of life that you are working so hard to put behind you. So how do you as a transsexual learn the gender-associated aspects of behavior required for a successful transition when all of society continuously works to instill the gender behaviors of your birth gender in you? There is no single, easy answer to this problem.

Prior to living full-time, observation of other people within your new gender is critical. Watch and learn as much as possible. Do not focus solely on appearance. Set your focus on what people do in response to the stimuli around them. People instinctively react to almost all little things in life and their actions are very often gender appropriate. How do men and women make requests of people? How do men and women interact in semi-private places such as public restrooms? When people get jammed together in a crowd, how do they collectively decide who goes first? At work, what is the difference in the management styles of male managers versus female managers? How do women collectively work together on projects versus men? In conflicts that arise inside or outside the home, how do women react differently from men facing the same conflict? Do not expect to see the same response to every situation, as people are unique. However, if you watch enough people, you will be able to see that most people react in a relatively consistent manner and be able to figure out the norms.

As you start living full-time and people start accepting you as a member of your identified gender, they will start treating you differently in many gender-specific ways. They will also expect you to start acting in gender-appropriate ways in response to their actions. Again, you have to be observant as they may send off cues that what you did was not appropriate. Just look for that totally confused look upon people's faces, and you will know you screwed up.

It is just like when you were a small child. You had so much opportunity to do inappropriate things when you were young because you just did not know any better. People reacted to what you did. They laughed at, frowned upon and scolded you, and you learned from your mistakes. It is no different now except you are older and probably a bit more stubborn. Do not be an old dog that cannot learn new tricks. You must!

If you are lucky, early on you will become a good friend with someone of your identified gender who totally accepts you. This is where all your private lessons of friendship will occur. You will learn from this special person what appropriate personal conversation is; what behavior is appropriate in public between close friends of your new gender; and most importantly what people of your gender really think about on an entire range of subjects such as sex, dating, relationships, etc. If he or she is a good friend, you will be told when you are out of bounds, and he or she will give you chances to correct your behavior. As in passing, listen carefully to your new friend.

If you are into self-help, numerous books and magazines cover the full gamut of subjects from etiquette to inter-personal relationships. Most women's magazines and a number of men's periodicals cover situations that people commonly encounter at home, in the workplace or during social events. You are not the first person to experience everything you are experiencing. In this day and age, it is almost certain that someone has written a blog, an article, a book, or posted a web page on the Internet that explains how they handled some strange or difficult situation that you are now experiencing. Either you can learn from the mistakes of others or you can learn the hard way. The choice is yours, but either way you will learn.

Some things about behavior you are just going to have to learn on your own. Being transsexual may present situations that do not normally arise for genetic girls or guys. People who know that you are transgender may expect you to act at times male, other times as female, or worse, some weird mix of the two. You may find yourself not being able to vocalize something properly because your voice is not gender appropriate yet. You may feel forced to make up stories or lie about your past. Your reactions to people who are physically attracted to you may be both exciting and terrifying at the same time, making your responses confusing or hostile.

In the end, though, time is on your side, and you will learn how to act and behave in a gender appropriate manner. Hopefully, at some point all the people in your life will slowly accept you as a member of your new gender. However, in doing so, they will expect you to behave in gender appropriate ways. They will let you know when you do not. Sometimes they will be subtle. Other times they will be in your face about it. However, when they truly treat you as your new gender, including expecting you to act appropriately, you can feel satisfaction for having reached a major milestone of the transitioning journey.

Learning to fit in and learning the behavior that is appropriate for your identified gender is probably the one step of transitioning that is never complete. This is not a problem as long as you do not falsely expect it to be complete. Just hope that over time, you stop seeing fitting in as being a task of transitioning, and you instead start seeing fitting in as a normal part of life, just as you did before you began to transition.

GOING BROKE

Of all the ugly realities of transitioning, none seems to be worse than the impact that the lack of wealth has on someone who suffers from gender dysphoria. Most insurance carriers purposely recognize gender reassignment surgery as experimental and recognize facial feminization surgery and mastectomies as cosmetic in order to refuse payment of insurance claims. They thereby increase their own profitability at the costs of those suffering from gender dysphoria.

Most transsexuals, therefore, find the costs associated with transitioning squarely placed upon them. The person who wishes to transition in order to relieve his or herself from the pain of gender dysphoria generally must do so entirely with his or her own money. As many transsexuals find out, these medical costs are often so high that they cannot begin to transition, they cannot transition in a timely manner, or they can only partially transition. The staggering costs of transitioning leave many transsexuals permanently feeling the pain of gender dysphoria. As a result, countless transsexuals suffer from ridicule and discrimination, in some cases for possibly the rest of their lives, due to their inability to alter their bodies sufficiently to remove the gender cues that prevent them from appearing to be members of their identified gender.

The failure of the medical insurance complex to cover the extreme costs of transitioning often creates two classes in society: those who are wealthy enough to treat their gender dysphoria and those who cannot. The lack of equitable insurance coverage causes there to be a split within the transsexual community, usually with the split following racial lines and the associated poverty that is often associated with being non-Caucasian in America and other countries.

If you think you can somehow handle the financial burden of transitioning, you will need to understand the costs associated with transitioning, the requirements imposed by the medical / psychological community prior to undergoing Gender Reassignment Surgery (GRS), and the medical steps you will be required to undertake so that you may live a relatively normal life post-transition.

The minimal requirements for transitioning as defined in the *Standards of Care* are twelve months of continuous hormonal therapy and twelve months of continuous living in the identified gender, also known as the Real-Life Experience. Fortunately, these two twelve-month periods can overlap. However, prior to starting hormone therapy, a minimum of three months of psychiatric counseling is required, and the *Standards of Care* expects this counseling to last throughout the Real-Life Experience.

The minimal financial burden that a transsexual must incur prior to undergoing gender reassignment is the cost of fifteen months of counseling, twelve months of hormone therapy, and the cost of a new wardrobe. Fortunately, mental health insurance coverage often includes counseling for gender dysphoria patients if billed as treatment for depression, anxiety, or stress management. If the transitioning person, however, does not have mental health coverage, counseling costs[14] alone can easily reach $9,100[15], if not more, during this period. For those without prescription drug coverage, the cost of hormones, anti-androgens and other prescription medications can range from a low of $1,680, to a high of $6,000[16] per year.

---

[14] All costs in this book are based in United States dollars at the start of 2009.

[15] The $9,100 counseling cost is calculated using an hourly counseling fee of $140/week for a period of 65 weeks.

[16] The $1,680 cost of prescription medication is based upon 12 months of estradiol and spironolactone at typical dosages, with each costing

Unless you were born with an incredibly perfect face and body that matches your gender identity, or you have no cares about your outward appearance in your new gender, there are going to be a fair number of ancillary charges that can add up quite quickly in addition to the minimal costs.

For a transwoman, these charges may include costs for facial hair removal and possibly body hair removal. Depending on the surgeon chosen to perform gender reassignment surgery, she may additionally require genital hair removal. As hormones do not change a male voice to female, she may need voice therapy to learn pitch and resonance, female voice characteristics, and feminine speaking patterns. If male pattern baldness or excessive hair thinning began prior to transitioning, she may need to purchase wigs and / or hair growth medications, and she may need hair transplants to fill in her bald spots. For some transwomen, hormone usage does not result in decent breast growth, and consequently, they may need to undertake breast augmentation surgery to increase the size of their breasts. Many transwomen also have one or more secondary gender characteristics of the face that they wish to have corrected via facial feminization surgery.

For a transman, there are less ancillary changes required due to the powerful body changing affects of the male sex hormone testosterone. Testosterone can cause the development of secondary gender characteristics of the face, lowering of the voice, facial and body hair growth, along with other body changes. Testosterone therapy, however, does not eliminate female breasts, and many transmen undergo removal of both breasts for the purposes of creating a well-defined male chest. Some transmen may undertake voice therapy to help learn male speech patterns.

---

approximately $70/month. Testosterone therapy via injection costs $100-$200/mo or $1,200-2,400/yr. Testosterone patches and gels typically cost $200-$500/mo, or $2,400-$6,000/yr.

When the costs of gender reassignment surgery are added to the required preparatory costs and the ancillary costs, the cost of changing one's body to match their gender identity can run anywhere from a low of $20,000 to well above $150,000. In my own case, psychotherapy, voice therapy, two facial feminization surgeries, facial laser hair removal, genital electrolysis, breast augmentation, vaginaplasty, labiaplasty and medical travel costs combined cost just a tad over $102,000 over a three-year period. Yes, if you have not yet figured this out, transitioning really does hurt the financial picture.

Beyond the obvious costs of transitioning are some not so obvious costs. As so many marriages fail as the result of a transsexual person initiating a transition, there can be quite a number of costs associated with legal fees for a divorce, alimony, and monthly child support payments. Divorce generally results in one or both parties leaving the family home. If the transitioning person leaves the family home, there will be moving costs, and costs associated with the acquisition of another home or the renting of an apartment. If the non-transitioning spouse leaves the family home, the transitioning spouse may incur the cost of refinancing the home so that the exiting spouse can receive the financial interests she or he holds in the home in cash. As a spouse that leaves may have had a large financial interest in the family home, mortgage payments may go up considerably following a divorce.

Divorce also generally results in the equal division of joint assets including half of any money saved for transitioning expenses. Following a divorce, there may be additional costs for obtaining new furnishings and possibly new transportation.

An unexpected cost for a transitioning person may be the cost of obtaining health insurance coverage following a divorce. It is easy to overlook the fact that an ex-spouse may be providing health and dental insurance coverage through his or her employer. This insurance coverage may suddenly terminate when a divorce becomes final. Obtaining new insurance may be especially costly if the transgender person's own employment benefit package is insufficient, the transgender person does not qualify for work related benefits, or there exists a pre-existing health care condition that places the transitioning person in a high-risk category when he or she attempts to obtain private health insurance.

As transitioning carries a risk of loss of employment, there is a fair risk depending on all the work-related factors discussed earlier of losing all income. A loss of employment can very easily completely stall a transition as the lack of income may make it entirely impossible to finance reassignment surgery, a mastectomy, or facial feminization surgery. Even if a transitioning person saves sufficient funds to qualify for surgery prior to a loss of employment, the costs of obtaining the essential necessities of life such as food and housing while new employment is being sought may eat away considerably at those savings. This may delay surgeries for indefinite periods of time.

If you lose your job and subsequently obtain new employment with an employer that is tolerant of gender variant people, you may incur additional commuting and relocation costs. You may possibly start your new job with a lower salary due to a loss of seniority or a lack of work experience in the new position.

For transwomen in particular, living as a woman carries with it the same prejudices afforded to genetic women in the workplace including reduced pay and lack of advancement opportunities. A transwoman may immediately experience these overlooked costs if she obtains new employment, and these overlooked costs may be long lasting regardless of whether a change of employer occurs or not.

Employees, though, are not the only workers whom a transition may financially damage. Independent researchers and contract employees may also experience prejudice in the awarding of research grants and consulting contracts. They may find that they are no longer awarded grants, or they may find the grants that they are awarded are for a lower value. Consultants may find their contracts are not renewed, work assignments may become menial or demeaning, or there may be far more down time between contracting assignments.

When you add all of the costs of transitioning together, including possible loss of income and divorce costs, the final costs of finding relief for the dysphoria associated with an incongruent gender identity may well turn out to be several hundred thousand dollars. For the lucky, however, the costs could be as little as $20,000. Actual costs are going to vary by individual. The hidden costs of transitioning most likely will affect older individuals with established families.

Financial planning and discipline is therefore a necessity to a successful transition. Not having the funds to obtain all the required medical services one needs can have an incredible emotional toll and a direct affect on the quality of life during and after the transition. Therefore, the transitioning person must maintain a sufficient income stream, must save substantial amounts of money on a regular basis, and in some cases may have to repair his or her credit history prior to starting a transition.

As society progresses, though, more and more employers in both the private and public sectors are starting to offer health insurance policies that include coverage for counseling costs, hormones, and in some cases reassignment surgery. Most insurance plans, however, still do not cover facial feminization surgery, mastectomies for gender transition purposes, or other surgeries that insurers may wrongly consider cosmetic. There may be, however, a tax deduction available for procedures that are medically necessary to relieve gender dysphoria.

Besides saving large sums for reassignment surgery, there may be ways to finance the transitioning costs over several years or essentially over a lifetime. If the transitioning person owns a home, he or she can possibly obtain a home equity line of credit or home equity loan. Alternatively, instead of taking a second loan against the property, he or she can refinance the property and take additional cash at settlement. If a home is not owned, he or she may be able to obtain a personal loan from financial institutions or supportive family members.

Being flexible in your choice of health care providers (e.g. surgeons) may also be an option for reducing costs. Costs for gender reassignment surgery are often lower outside of the United States. In Thailand, the cost of gender reassignment surgery can be 50% less than the costs of an equivalent surgery that occurs within the U.S. Additionally, both within and outside the U.S. there may also be health care providers that implement a sliding scale fee schedule that is dependent upon the patient's financial status and ability to pay.

If the costs of transitioning give you sticker shock, do not lose all hope. Planning, determination, financial discipline and creativeness are just some of the attributes each transitioning person needs to develop to make it through the minefield of transition finances. The goal of being able to have reassignment surgery is achievable for most people regardless of their financial status. If one is willing and able to exercise financial discipline, save regularly over a long period, work hard to make extra cash, and remain patient enough to follow through with his or her transition plans even though at times transitioning seems to be a financial impossibility, then the financial challenges that face a transition can be conquered. Thousands of transsexual people transition every year, and they are not all rich. So do not lose hope. Work hard to make your dreams become realities.

LEGALITIES

After you have figured out that you can handle the stresses of coming out to family and friends, finance your transition, and prepared yourself to start the Real-Life Experience, you may think you have transitioning all figured out. No transition, however, is truly complete until you have fully experienced the joys of government bureaucracy and the workings of the judicial system. Regardless of how much you would like to avoid dealing with the legal system or government agencies in general, you cannot avoid legalities and bureaucracy when you transition.

If you are following the WPATH *Standards of Care* for your transition, you are required to legally adopt a gender-appropriate first name. Although this is a technically just a requirement, legally changing your name is truly a major milestone in your transition. It is very symbolic of your commitment to follow through with your transition. Fulfilling the name change requirement thus becomes one of the first legal issues you will want to and need to address during your transition.

You may believe that changing your name should be a simple process and if you are lucky, your name change will be just that. Depending upon where you live, though, you may find that changing your name may not be all that trivial.

Typically, you obtain a legal name change by filing a petition with a local or state court that requests the court legally recognize the name you wish to adopt. The courts, however, in wanting to prevent name changes from being used as mechanisms of fraud, often make the name change process intentionally cumbersome to insure the public is properly notified prior to allowing a name change to occur. While some jurisdictions will allow a judge to summarily order a name change with no public notice, many jurisdictions require posting of a legal notice on the courthouse door or in a local newspaper for days or weeks.

If you live in an area that is not transgender friendly, having a legal notice run in the local paper or posted at the courthouse that says you are changing your male name to a female name, or vice-versa, as part of a gender transition can really be a bit unnerving. Who will see the notice? Who will discover you are transitioning that you do not wish to know yet? Will it be your boss, a co-worker or a member of your church? You just do not know who will see the notice of your name change.

Therefore, the timing of a legal name change has to be a serious consideration for you. You should not start the legal proceedings until you are ready to live fulltime in your new gender. If you file your name change petition too soon and you have not yet finished coming out to the important people in your life such as your family or your employer, your name change may suddenly force you into an awkward position at an inopportune time.

Alternatively, if you hold off too long to legally change your name, you may find that your employer may not want to start using your new name in the workplace prior to finalization of your legal name change. While this action by your employer may seem unreasonable to you, your employer will have to change your payroll data, notify insurance carriers, modify computer accounts, create a new employee badge, purchase new business cards, etc. to accommodate your name change. Some of the changes that your employer will be making on your behalf can only be made after you have obtained a legal name change order.

In trying to determine the best time to initiate a legal name change, do not forget that maintaining employment and financial stability is extremely critical during your transition. This means that if you are employed, you should tightly couple the timing of your name change and coming out at work.

You do not want to find yourself in the position of looking for a new job in a non-transgender-friendly area with a legal name that does not match your current gender. By holding off on legally changing your name until after you notify your current employer of your transition plans, you retain the ability to find a new job in your birth gender, using your birth name, should the disclosure to your current employer make you unemployed.

Timing considerations aside, a caveat to getting a legal name change is that not all jurisdictions permit a person to adopt a name that does not match his or her birth gender. In jurisdictions in which laws, legal precedence, or judicial prejudice prevent a person from choosing any name for his or herself, a petitioner to the court may find that he or she is dealing with a court that refuses to grant a name change for a name that is "not appropriate" for the petitioner's birth gender.

To reduce the risk that a court will refuse your petition for name change, consider legal venue shopping before you file your petition for a name change. In other words, try to file your petition for a name change, or any other petition to the court related to your transition, in a jurisdiction that you know issues favorable decisions towards transgender people. For instance, while most states currently do not have ordinances that protect gender identity or expression, most states do have at least one large municipality that does. If you are able to file your petitions to a court within one of these municipalities, you should have a much better chance of getting your petition granted.

If you are planning to eventually live in stealth or pseudo-stealth, you may find that use of a name change court order will draw attention to the fact that you are a transsexual. Obtaining an amended birth certificate that has your new name and new gender after reassignment surgery will prevent you from having to out yourself as being transsexual at critical times in your life. A primary example, for instance, would be applying for a new job.

Like name changes, amending birth certificates can be easy or tricky depending upon where you live. Some jurisdictions will allow the amendment of a birth certificate by simply filling out a birth certificate amendment application, and submitting the application along with the court orders that change your name and gender to the state agency that manages birth certificates. Other jurisdictions require that you file suit in court against the agency that manages birth records, requesting in the suit that the court order the agency named in the complaint to amend your birth certificate. Unfortunately, some places still completely prohibit the amendment of birth records.

If the state or country in which you were born requires a court to order the amendment of your birth certificate, you may find that the state or country in which you currently reside does not have jurisdiction to make such an order. For instance, the court in one state cannot order the bureau of vital records in another state to amend a birth certificate. If this situation applies to you, you may need to file suit against the regulatory agency in your birth state, which may significantly add to your legal costs.

Once you do obtain your legal name change and optionally amend the name on your birth certificate, you need to change your name on every financial account, insurance plan, vehicle and property title, license, etc. issued under your birth name. For most people, though, the first document they want to change after obtaining a name change order is their driver's license as this is the most commonly used form of legal identification. Luckily, changing your name on your driver's license is generally not hard. Typically, you just present the court order for name change to your local motor vehicle administration along with your existing license, and the motor vehicle administration creates a new driver's license with your new name.

Nevertheless, as a transitioning transsexual, do you really desire having a driver's license that has your new name and your birth gender during the Real-Life Experience period? Of course not. It would be safer for you if your new license were to contain both your identified gender and your new legal name. The ability to change a gender marker on a driver's license prior to undergoing reassignment surgery, though, varies from state to state. The states that do allow a temporary gender marker change to occur before reassignment surgery generally have a fairly complex process that has to be muddled through. This may require you to prove to a state agency, a bureaucracy, that you are a "real" transsexual in the process of transitioning. Regardless of how complex that process is, obtaining a temporary gender marker change on a license is well worth all of the effort that you put into it.

The advantage of getting the gender marker changed on your driver's license during the Real-Life Experience is that you reduce the chance of triggering discriminating behaviors from people who have a reasonable need to check your driver's license. This includes police officers, bouncers at clubs, and clerks at local stores who demand to see your license for proof of age or proof of identity when you use your credit card or write checks in their establishments. If someone in the wrong place sees your birth gender when you present your license, you may find yourself suddenly becoming a target of discrimination or violence. This is especially true if you frequent bars or nightclubs in a very conservative area[17].

Getting the gender marker temporarily changed on your driver's license before undergoing reassignment surgery does not automatically make you a member of your identified gender from a legal viewpoint. In the eyes of the law, you are still your birth gender, and the temporary gender marker change on your license is simply a courtesy that the state is making to improve your quality of life and to reduce the risk of harm befalling you.

Consequentially, if you find yourself incarcerated, having a temporary gender marker on your license is going to have little effect on which prison, male or female, prison officials will house you. Prison officials will most likely house you based upon your genitals or the gender on your birth certificate, and not the gender marker on your driver's license. If you are lucky, you may find yourself placed in a

---

[17] If you truly feel that you may incur bodily injury as a result of being accidentally outed as a transsexual in a bar or nightclub you desire to go to, use common sense and go some place safer. Alcohol and bigotry do not mix well!

protective unit, but the odds are you are going to be at great risk if prison officials place you in a general population unit that matches your birth gender. Even if you can get a lawyer to seek a protective order that changes your housing situation, other prisoners may abuse or rape you during the weeks or months that go by before a judge issues such an order. Living fulltime, therefore, is a period of your life where you really have to be certain not to do anything that will result in imprisonment.

However, living as a member of your identified gender during the Real-Life Experience means you will have to use at times facilities that match your identified gender. Depending upon where you live, using a public facility such as a dressing room or bathroom that does not match your physical / legal gender may be illegal, and you may be putting yourself at risk of being arrested. If someone does make an issue of you using a public facility that he or she does not believe you should be using, presenting a driver's license with a temporary gender marker change may allow you to quickly quell a challenge to your right to use the facility in question.

In addition to a temporary gender marker change, you may wish to obtain and keep in your possession a "carry letter". A carry letter is a letter written by a therapist that attests that the person carrying the letter is transsexual, is in the process of transitioning, and is medically required to live as the gender opposite of his or her birth gender as part of his or her treatment for gender dysphoria. Carry letters usually ask that the person reading the letter grant the transitioning person the same rights and privileges that a member of the gender that the transsexual is transitioning to is granted. While a carry letter has no legal authority that permits the holder to use facilities of his or her identified gender, it may motivate some law enforcement officers or judges to grant you some leeway should you find yourself in the position of defending your usage of gender specific facilities.

Completing reassignment surgery of course truly makes you a member of your identified gender. However, in the eyes of the law you are still a member of your birth gender until you either amend your birth certificate to reflect your new gender, or get a court order that orders that you surgically changed your sex. Some jurisdictions, though, sadly do not recognize that a person can ever change his or her sex by surgical procedure.

If you find yourself seeking a court order for change of gender but are unable to obtain such an order where you were born, you may have other legal avenues that give you the proper legal status following reassignment surgery. For instance, the courts in my home state do not have the authority to order another state to amend the sex on a birth certificate. However, these courts do have the authority to issue a court order that orders the petitioner has had his or her gender surgically altered, and that the petitioner's sex be the new gender. A person who obtains a court order of this kind can use the order, in lieu of a birth certificate, to prove his or her gender.

If you live in the United States and find you are having trouble getting the local courts to issue an order that legally makes you your post-operative sex, you may find the easiest legal document for you to obtain with an appropriate gender marker is, surprisingly, from the federal government. For a very reasonable fee, the Department of State can issue you a new passport with an appropriate gender marker by simply submitting a copy of a certified letter issued by the surgeon who performed your gender change procedure along with a passport application. Once the government issues a new passport, you can use it to get other legal documents changed such as social security records, etc.

Some people that undergo reassignment surgery do not wish to obtain a court order changing their gender. Usually this is the case for people who are not certain of where their sexual orientation lies following surgery. If a post-operative transsexual finds himself or herself in a same-sex relationship following reassignment surgery, *not* obtaining a court ordered gender change order or amended birth certificate may provide certain legal protections. First, if the person is in an established marriage, not getting a court order or amended birth certificate may create a defense against a person or entity that challenges the validity of the marriage should there be a local prohibition on same-sex marriages. Secondly, delaying the legal gender change may allow two same-sex people to enter into a same-sex marriage in a jurisdiction that prohibits same-sex marriages.

Not acquiring a court order for gender change or an amended birth certificate can be very risky. The risks associated with incarceration that exist during the Real-Life Experience period also exist after reassignment surgery if there has not been a legal gender change. Lack of a court ordered gender change or amended birth certificate may result in prison officials housing a post-operative transwoman in a male housing unit, or a transman in a female housing unit, if prison officials use birth records or legal sex to determine housing. As during the Real-Life Experience, the best solution for this problem, of course, is to stay out of the criminal justice system and out of prison.

Another overlooked factor that you need to consider while obtaining a court order for a gender or name change is that court proceedings leave an audit trail that you underwent a gender change. As more and more court systems place these records online, you may find that anyone with access to the Internet can find out that you are transsexual even if you pass completely as a member of your new gender. If you do file a name or gender change petition with the court, you may wish to get an additional court order that seals the name and gender change court records, and prohibits the electronic posting of related case information on the Internet.

As mentioned earlier, if you successfully undergo reassignment surgery while married, you may find that your change of gender has placed you into a same-sex marriage. In jurisdictions that prohibit same-sex marriages, you may find your gender change placed you into an area of law that has not yet been determined. Legal questions such as "Is the marriage still valid?", "Is the marriage automatically annulled?", or even "Is the marriage even a same-sex marriage at all?" have to be determined by the courts if someone challenges the validity of your marriage, or your entitlement to marital rights and privileges.

If you are unmarried or divorced following GRS and wish to get married at some later point in life, you may find yourself prohibited from doing so. Determination of gender with respect to marriage varies state by state, and country by country. Some locals may base gender for purposes of marriage on genetics, some may make the determination using post-surgical gender, and some may make the determination using identified gender. Some locales that have laws based on religious doctrines, or that still have officials who follow their strong religious beliefs may restrict a transsexual from ever marrying anyone of either sex.

Regardless of whether a transsexual undergoes GRS or obtains legal recognition of a new gender *after* GRS, the fact that someone is transsexual may be used in court proceedings, such as custody battles, to bias the court against the transgender party. Another area of law where the bias of being transsexual comes into play is in the awarding of alimony during a divorce. In some jurisdictions, statutes permit the family courts to look at the cause of a divorce when granting alimony and calculating the size of alimony awards. Hence, the judge may see a decision to transition as a legal basis to award alimony, or as a basis for awarding a larger alimony payment to the non-transitioning spouse.

As many, if not all, of the legal issues presented up to this point may require you to seek legal representation, a word of caution has to be given here about choosing legal professionals to protect your legal interests. If you seek legal assistance, you may find that many lawyers have biases against transsexuals even though they accept transsexuals as their clients. Lawyers are human like everyone else, and their ignorance concerning transsexuality may cause them to project their own prejudices onto how cases or trials may be resolved by the courts. Insomuch, they may provide unsound legal advice, recommend that a person settle for a lesser amount in a civil proceeding, or even suggest that a transgender defendant take an unjust plea deal in a criminal trial.

You may also find that many lawyers, even those that promote themselves as LGBT lawyers, are also unsure of transgender law, as this is a rapidly changing field of law, and a field of law that many lawyers have not practiced. If you need to hire a lawyer to represent you in a case involving a divorce, child custody or employment discrimination, it is crucial that you find a lawyer who is not biased, and who can properly represent you in the face of attempts to bias the court against you. It is critically important that any lawyer you hire know the legal rights and protections that you, as a transsexual, *do or do not have* in the jurisdiction in which he or she will represent you.

Even if you do not think you need a lawyer for any civil or criminal issues, you may find that you need the services of a good lawyer prior to undergoing surgical procedures such as GRS and FFS (facial feminization surgery). These surgical procedures are not just minor outpatient procedures. The risks of surgery and the consequences should something go wrong, should never be discounted.

When you undertake any surgery, no matter how small, you are risking your life. You can never be sure you will not have a negative reaction to anesthesia. You can never be sure your body will be able to handle the stresses placed upon it by the surgical procedure or the ensuing recovery. Moreover, you can never be sure your surgeon will not make a serious error, including one that may take your life.

Therefore, prior to undergoing any surgery, you should make sure you have a competent lawyer draw up a final will. You should also have a lawyer create documents that establish a durable power of attorney for medical decisions while you are undergoing surgical procedures. In addition, you should establish a durable power of attorney to handle the finances of your estate should any problem that arises during your surgeries leave you incapacitated.

Depending upon where you live and where you have your surgery, you may need to establish a living will that specifies the level of medical care you wish to receive if something terribly wrong occurs during surgery. The person who will make medical decisions for you should have no doubts about what, if any, level of advanced life support you desire should anything go awry during these procedures.

However, if you are undergoing GRS or FFS in a foreign country, the documents you establish in your home country that specify your legal wishes, such as advanced medical directives, may not be legally binding in the country in which you are having the surgery performed. If this is the case for you, prior to undergoing surgery, you should determine who will be allowed to make medical decisions on your behalf in the country where your surgical procedures will take place, and what options will be available to him or her. For instance, will the person you chose to be your guardian be able to take you off a respirator or have a feeding tube removed? Will he or she be able to send you home or to another country so you can receive more advanced health care?

We all like to think the surgeons we choose to do our surgeries are the best in world and never make errors. But to err is human, and doctors err all the time. Therefore, you should research and resolve all the issues of living wills, final wills, and advanced medical directives prior to committing yourself to a specific surgeon. The consequences may be dire for you and your family should something go wrong. Do not overlook the risks of surgery in your rush to change gender.

One final note regarding legalities: Do not completely overlook the costs of legal representation while planning your transition. A good lawyer can be very costly. Even if you plan to file your own name and gender change petitions directly with the court, there will be filing fees and fees associated with the posting of legal notices if your jurisdiction requires them. Additional costs may be realized when you go to get new forms of identification (I replaced my license four times during my transition), request a new passport, or request duplicates of legal documents such as court orders and birth certificates.

PHYSICAL ASPECTS OF TRANSITIONING

The obvious reason why someone undergoes a gender transition is to make his or her physical gender match his or her gender identity. From a more human viewpoint, the not so obvious reason for undergoing a transition is simply to make the pain of having an incongruent gender go away. When you make enough changes to your body and life that the pain and anguish of having a gender mismatch are no longer an issue for you, then you will have succeeded in your transition.

Nevertheless, many transsexuals mistakenly believe that having gender reassignment surgery alone will solve all their woes. GRS by itself is not a solution to the problem of living successfully in your identified gender. As you go through the transition process, you will find yourself constantly confronted with several nagging questions. When you look in the mirror, are you comfortable with your face and body? When you go out and meet the public, do you feel those whom you encounter truly accept you as a member of your identified gender? Do you feel attractive to others, both in sexual and non-sexual ways? Do you feel embarrassed or awkward when you meet new people or leave the confines of your safe zone? Do the people around you make you feel less than human because of your appearance?

The questions above hit at the root of two core issues, the first being whether you accept yourself and the second being whether you are accepted in your identified gender by family, friends and the rest of society. The answers to these questions can be very painful if the physical changes you undergo as you transition are poorly done, incomplete, or omitted.

If post-GRS you cannot look in the mirror everyday without despising your appearance, what have you accomplished by having reassignment surgery? Absolutely nothing. **Reassignment surgery in itself is not a cure for the pain and suffering of having an incongruent gender identity, if you still feel the pain of gender dysphoria following completion of the procedure.**

Too many transgender people rush to a gender surgeon as the first step or second step of the physical transition process. They save up enough money for a reasonably affordable GRS surgeon, get minimal psychological counseling, start on hormones and then rush off for reassignment surgery. Afterwards, when they come home, they find out that although they can now legally change their gender on their birth certificates, no one they encounter honestly believes they are truly women or men. They find that life remains painful each time others reject, ridicule, or discriminate against them because of their mixed appearance.

If you cannot honestly answer "better" to the question "Will my life be better or worse after the procedures I'm planning to have?", you should not undergo any physical modifications until you can. You must fully understand the consequences of not completing all the physical changes that you as a unique person require to live successfully in your identified gender, or you may find yourself wishing you never transitioned.

To find inner peace, you have to feel comfortable with your self-image. If you are a transwoman and you hate the male characteristics of your face, everyday of your post-GRS life will be painful unless you remove those persistent male characteristics from your face that developed during puberty. You can go through life telling everyone you know that you are happy that you switched your gender, but if you do not believe deep down inside that you are complete in your changes you will never find inner peace.

I cannot tell you in a book which combination of physical changes you specifically will have to undergo to have a successful transition.

Every person is unique in his or her appearance. Due to this fact, each person needs to tailor his or her physical changes to match his or her unique body and face. Please be honest with yourself. Get undressed and look at your face and body in a set of full-length mirrors so you can see yourself from all angles. Are the reflections that you see of yourself the reflections you want to see at the end of your transition? If they are not, what physical changes must you make to be sufficiently feminine or masculine at the end of your transition to relieve you of your gender dysphoria? Then get dressed and stand in front of those mirrors again. Do you really look appropriate for your new gender when you are dressed normally? If not, what in particular is wrong with your appearance and what can be done to change each of the things that continues to make you look like a member of your birth gender? Finally, concentrate solely on the image of your face in the mirror.

I cannot emphasize enough how much attention you need to pay to your facial characteristics. People do not see what is in your pants or under your skirt except when you are in private. The first time someone sees your face he or she immediately assigns you as being either male or female. If you have beautiful breasts as results of undergoing breast augmentation and the most realistic looking vagina that a surgeon can create, people will still read you as male if you have a five o'clock shadow, brow bossing, or a "male" jaw line. As a result, everywhere you go there will always be the problem of being read, possibly being embarrassed, harassed or discriminated against because of your facial features.

So read on and decide which physical changes you will have to undergo **before** deciding to take hormones and **before** you start to transition. If you cannot make all of the changes that you need to live successfully as a woman or man, your life after the transition process may be far worse than it was before you started your transition. This is not what anyone wants. Be honest about your appearance and your feelings. Evaluate yourself from head to toe, making sure you consider carefully all of the areas of your body and appearance that may affect your quality of life after transitioning.

Do not overlook the fact that your personal finances may strongly affect the physical changes you are going to be allowed to undertake and when. Younger transgender people in particular may experience very long delays between surgical procedures because of their limited incomes. Because these waits may last for years, be honest with yourself when prioritizing the order of your surgical procedures.

For instance, if you have difficulties passing due to your facial gender cues, will you be comfortable living day to day if you have GRS as your first major surgical procedure but cannot afford FFS for the next five years? On the other hand, if you opt for FFS first, will you be able to endure the pain of having male genitalia while you save up for GRS? You need to do a lot of soul searching in order to arrive at a sequence that will satisfy your unique needs.

The order that made the best sense for me was to simultaneously start growing out my hair, undergo laser hair removal of my facial hair and begin speech therapy to learn to speak properly. I then underwent two facial feminization surgeries. One year later, I underwent both breast augmentation and gender reassignment surgeries at the same time. This made the most sense for me, as I wanted to be able to live with minimal discrimination during my Real-Life Experience, and I wanted to feel comfortable with myself while I awaited GRS.

The order of my changes, though, is unique to my financial situation and my particular needs. I have a very healthy head of hair and did not need a hair transplant. You may need to add that into your plans. You may be younger and not need as much facial hair removed. If you are overweight, you may have to include time in your schedule to lose weight as many surgeons have weight limits when accepting patients for surgery. If you smoke, smoking can affect the ability of wounds to heal and you may be required to give up smoking before undergoing facial and reassignment surgeries. If you have lost a lot of weight prior to transitioning, you may have to calculate in the costs of other cosmetic surgeries such as a tummy tuck or a face-lift.

Only you truly know what set of changes you must make to relieve yourself of the gender dysphoria that you experience. Do not, however, become addicted to making body modifications. No matter how hard you try, the odds are you will never be entirely male or female in every aspect of your physical appearance. There are just too many secondary sex characteristics (e.g. pelvic size, feet size, height, etc.) that you cannot have surgically corrected. Plan to make the changes you need, but at some point in your plan make sure there exists a definitive end to the body and face modifications that you intend to make.

HAIR

When a transwoman starts her transition, one of the first items she will most likely have to address will be her hair. If she has excessive body hair due to having male hormones and the genes she inherited, she will have to start the long process of controlling it. If the same hormones and genetics are causing her head hair to thin, recede or vanish, everyday that goes by without arresting that hair loss will increase the burden she will have to undertake to ensure a feminine head of hair at the end of her transition. Her facial hair, if any, will have to be completely removed to guarantee a feminine appearance. Therefore, she has to consider the treatment of her hair over her entire body, from head to toe, during the transition process.

Surprisingly leg, arm and torso hair is often very easy to manage for a transwoman. While many transwomen believe they will need laser hair removal or electrolysis over their entire bodies, they quickly find the reduction in testosterone that occurs as they transition reduces significantly hair growth on the torso, and causes their body hair to thin and become softer. Periodic shaving or the use of depilatories is often all that they need to do to manage leg, arm or torso hair.

Facial hair, unfortunately, is much harder than body hair to manage for the average person. Reducing testosterone medically or surgically does not reduce facial hair, forcing most transwomen to undergo electrolysis and / or laser hair removal, both of which are greatly misunderstood.

Both laser and electrolysis are painful, expensive and time consuming. Most people have an initial misconception that a single laser session or a few electrolysis sessions will permanently remove all the hair they want removed. Hair, unfortunately, grows in cycles and removal must occur over a long period of time, preferably while it is in its early growth phase.

Typically, the period of time it takes to remove facial hair is generally not less than 35 weeks long[18]. Sometimes, however, facial hair removal may take well over a year to complete, considerably delaying some aggressive transition plans. Laser hair removal also has limited efficacy with lighter hair colors and darker skin tones. Electrolysis, even if not the first choice for many transwomen, is often needed to completely remove the hairs not removed by the laser hair removal process.

The benefit that laser hair removal has over electrolysis is that it takes on average six to twelve sessions, lasting less than an hour each, with sessions spaced approximately seven weeks apart. Resultantly, the six to twelve hours spent in treatment for laser is significantly less than the possibly hundreds of hours required to completely remove facial hair via electrolysis. Laser hair removal also requires the face to be well shaven before each session, which is a benefit to any transwoman living full or part-time as a woman. Electrolysis, unfortunately, requires facial hair to be long enough to be seen and

---

[18] Many laser hair removal providers recommend that at least six laser sessions be undertaken no less than seven weeks apart. Following the initial six sessions, follow up sessions are often needed to remove hair that did not respond well to the first set of treatments. This can take four or five additional treatments, each seven weeks apart. Finally, hair not removed by laser treatments must be removed by electrolysis over a several month period. Ouch...

grabbed with tweezers, which can be a real issue for transwomen with dark facial hairs and who do not want to be seen publicly for a couple of days before each session with a partial beard or mustache.

The downside to laser hair removal is that it may not permanently remove hair. In some instances, laser hair removal may only cause a temporary reduction of hair. Laser treatments may also cause permanent discoloration of the skin for people with higher levels of pigment in their skin. Laser hair removal is contraindicated for people with a history of seizures and other medical conditions. You need to assess both electrolysis and laser, like any other medical procedure, for risks and complications before beginning treatments.

While many people believe that only transwomen seek the services of an electrologist during a transition, transmen preparing for a phalloplasty may also need to undergo hair removal prior to gender reassignment surgery. A phalloplasty, which is one of the FTM reassignment surgeries described below in more detail, uses skin taken from other parts of the body such as the forearms, the groin area, the side of the torso, or the legs to construct a penis. To prevent unwanted hair from growing in places where it should not after surgery, many surgeons ask that their patients prepare for a phalloplasty by having all of the hair removed from the area that the surgeon plans to use as the tissue source for the penis. Transmen who do not heed this request may be required to use depilatories or other methods of hair removal on a regular basis after the completion of reassignment surgery.

Although testosterone causes men to naturally develop facial and body hair, it interestingly and sadly leads to male pattern baldness and / or a recessed hairline near the temples in men as they age. For transwomen, their natural testosterone production prior to the start of hormone replacement therapy combined with their unique genetic makeup can cause significant head hair loss. Although taking anti-androgens often slows down or stops future hair loss in transwomen, hormone replacement therapy alone does not cause hair to re-grow in areas of the scalp that are hairless or where hair has thinned. In addition, even though hormone replacement therapy may stop future hair loss for some transwomen, genetics strongly influence several forms of hair loss, and resultant hair loss may continue well beyond the start of hormone therapy. This leaves many transwomen needing to have hair transplants, use hair extensions, or permanently wear wigs.

Many transwomen also report a loss or thinning of head hair following facial feminization surgery. Some people hypothesize that this thinning results from the extreme amounts of anesthesia absorbed by the body during the surgery[19], or damage to the scalp or hair follicles during the surgery itself if the frontal hairline is advanced. Often this hair loss is temporary, but it may be a serious consideration for someone with very thin hair prior to undergoing surgery.

For transmen, testosterone therapy can trigger male pattern baldness and receding hairlines soon after beginning hormone therapy. This may be a huge shock to a transman who always had a healthy head of hair and who was expecting to have that full head of hair throughout his life. And as noted previously, since testosterone levels greatly influence the production of body hair, many transmen find out way too late that those testosterone shots they have been taking have turned them into unusually hairy men. This is quite a shock for some transmen who dreamed of having healthy looking, hairless, well-sculpted, masculine bodies following their transitions.

One additional minor head hair difference between men and women that transsexuals often initially overlook is the distance from the eyebrows to the hairline. Men typically have a larger forehead than women do. Many transwomen choose to correct this by undergoing a scalp advancement procedure as part of facial feminization surgery. For transmen, testosterone and aging may cause the hairline to recede naturally over time allowing them to appear more masculine with age.

---

[19] Patients undergoing facial feminization surgery may be anesthetized for as long as twelve hours for a single surgery.

FACE

Your face is like a picture: it tells a thousand words about you to everyone who lays eyes upon you. Your face tells the world your heritage, your age, your ethnicity, and of course your gender. Each human face has so many gender cues that each of us immediately recognizes who is male and who is female just by looking at a person's face even though we may not be consciously aware that the process is occurring. In order to understand why people see you as either male or female, you have to understand the major structural differences of the face that exist between the sexes.

Starting with the forehead, the frontal sinuses are located above each eye, to the right and left of the bridge of the nose, and are covered by facial bones. When males go through puberty, the bones over the frontal sinus grow outward creating a prominence referred to as brow bossing. The amount of brow bossing varies from male to male. Brow bossing affects the general shape of the forehead, the angle of the upper eye orbits, and the perceived depth or "openness" of the eyes.

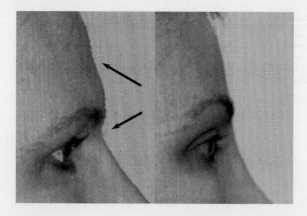

FIGURE 1 - BROW BOSSING (L), BROW BOSSING CORRECTED (R)

Women do not develop this prominent brow as a secondary sex characteristic. They generally have smoother and rounder foreheads. Their upper eye orbits appear more vertical than horizontal when viewed from the side, as the sinuses are not pushing out over the eyes. This results in eyes that appear more open, larger, visible and not as deeply recessed. Likewise, women's eyebrows typically sit high on the orbits and follow the rims of the orbits.

Moving down the face a bit, you will find noses also differ according to gender. Although noses vary from person to person and have shapes that ethnicity and genetics greatly influence, women generally have smaller noses than men of similar heritage do. Male noses tend to have larger, wider nostrils that project further from the face. Because of brow bossing, male noses often terminate abruptly between the eyes, whereas, female noses tend to flow smoothly into the forehead.

Left and right of the nose, women generally have cheekbones that are more prominent. Below the nose, men have considerably more skin between the upper lip and the bottom of the nose. This extra skin causes the upper lip in men to obscure partially the upper teeth when they smile or talk. Female lips generally are fuller and shapelier than male lips. The higher position of female lips on the face exposes more of a woman's upper teeth both during normal conversations and during a smile.

Moving down to the lower portion of the face, the jaw and chin define the bottom of the face for both men and women. For males, the jaw is larger; a product of thicker bones and stronger muscles, and the chin is squarer and has more vertical height. For women, the chin is typically rounder and shorter, and the jaw is tapered and more delicate.

Note that the statements above about faces are just generalizations. Both men and women have infinite variations in their faces and both may have features of the opposite sex present in their faces. You may already have features in your face of the gender with which you identify, but it is the sum of your features that dictates whether others will see your face as being female or male when they first catch glimpse of you.

For genetic males, the development of secondary male sex characteristics of the face results from the natural testosterone produced during puberty. A transman who went through puberty as a teenage girl and who takes testosterone during the transition process will see his face masculinize over time as if he went through puberty as a genetic male.

Unfortunately, if you are a transwomen, the estrogens and anti-androgens taken during hormone replacement therapy will not remove the secondary male sex characteristics of the face that developed during puberty. If you wish to remove the secondary sex characteristics of your face, you must undergo facial feminization surgery to trim and reshape the bones of your face that masculinized during your puberty. Although FFS is very expensive[20], FFS can have extremely positive effects on your ability to live in society without discrimination or harassment. On a positive note, you can make facial feminization surgical changes incrementally as finances permit. So do not lose hope when you see the estimate from a surgeon who specializes in facial feminization.

BODY

A person who has a gender that is congruent with his or her own gender identity typically finds it almost unfathomable that anyone would want to alter or remove his or her genitals to solve any emotional problem including gender dysphoria. However, for transsexuals, many a day passes in silent hope of that special morning when they wake to find they are no longer male or no longer female. They dream of that day God will grant them their lifelong wish to become a woman or to become a man. As Divine intervention of this nature does not occur on any regular basis, transsexuals turn to gifted surgeons who can modify the two primary areas of their bodies that require surgical modifications to relieve gender dysphoria: the breasts and the genitals.

---

[20] FFS typically costs between $20,000 and $50,000 as of 2009. Factors affecting the cost of FFS include choice of surgeon, types of procedures performed, number of procedures performed, hospital and post-recovery care fees, and transportation costs.

Breast tissue grows into breasts when a teenage girl undergoes breast development during puberty or when a transwoman undergoes hormone replacement therapy during her transition. If you are in the process of transitioning, you probably have found that you have too much breast tissue if you are a transman, or too little if you are a transwoman.

For a transman, undergoing a double mastectomy removes the breast tissue that developed during puberty. The surgeon who performs a double mastectomy for a transman typically performs additional procedures to contour the remaining chest tissue into a masculine appearing chest. A mastectomy with chest contouring can significantly improve a transman's ability to pass, while providing great improvements in both comfort and health.

The non-surgical alternative a transman has to reduce the impact of having breasts is to bind his breasts to give the impression of a flat male chest. While binding one's breasts may seem to be a simple solution to having developed breasts during puberty, binding can seriously damage the breasts or other organs if the binding is excessively tight. As binding is uncomfortable and constrictive, it may also negatively affect stamina and the ability to perform certain physical actions. From a psychological perspective, a transitioning transman may feel an increased level of gender dysphoria when he removes his binder each day and his body appears feminine once again. He may also have an increase in gender dysphoria if the binding does not sufficiently flatten his breasts, making him feel that his breasts are causing everyone he meets to read him as female.

For a transwoman, breast tissue does not develop naturally into breasts during puberty. However, the synthetic estrogens and anti-androgens she takes during hormone replacement therapy can cause breast development to occur. Unfortunately, the breast development that occurs as a product of hormone replacement therapy generally does not reach the same level of development that would have occurred had the transwoman been born female. Typically, a transwoman's breasts will grow to a size about one to two bra cup sizes smaller than her mother's or sisters' natural breast sizes. For some, this may be a very acceptable size, and for others the amount of breast tissue that develops will be too minimal for their breasts to ever appear feminine.

The surgical solution for small breasts is breast augmentation using saline or silicone gel implants. Breast augmentation surgery is a very common procedure for both natal and transsexual women. Non-surgical solutions for having small breasts include wearing padded push-up bras, using external silicone gel prosthesis, and taping of the breasts to give the appearance of more breast tissue than actually exists. A final option overlooked by many transwomen is just to live with small breasts. Not all women are naturally large breasted, and many women live happy, normal lives with the small breasts that naturally developed during puberty.

Down below the belt line, however, there are few non-surgical options to relieve gender dysphoria. As most people generally define a person's sex by his or her genitals, no option short of surgically reassigning one's sex will permanently relieve a person of his or her gender dysphoria.

The gender reassignment surgical options for transwomen are essentially limited to vaginaplasty and labiaplasty procedures. A transwoman can undergo a vaginaplasty to construct a fully functional vagina and sensate clitoris. Depending upon the surgeon, construction of the labia majora may occur at the same time the vagina is constructed, or construction of the labia majora may occur several months later as part of a separate labiaplasty procedure. As surgical techniques have improved greatly in recent years, an estimated 90% of transwoman who undergo a vaginaplasty are able to participate in sexual activities and reach sexual orgasm.

The primary reason reassignment surgery is so successful for transwomen is that there exists during surgery plenty of natural tissue to construct a vagina, clitoris and labia majora. Even a transwoman who does not have ample penile or scrotal tissue prior to reassignment surgery can optionally have skin harvested from her hips or lower belly during surgery to ensure the achievement of adequate vaginal depth. Moreover, the fact that the urethra is longer in genetic males than it is in females allows a surgeon to safely relocate the urethral opening to its anatomically correct position during a vaginaplasty procedure.

Some transwomen, for personal or financial reasons, optionally choose to not have a vagina surgically constructed. Instead, they opt to undergo an orchiectomy, a procedure that just removes their testicles. By undergoing this procedure, they experience a major decrease in their testosterone levels and remove the need to take anti-androgens as part of their daily hormone therapy regimens. In some rare instances, some transwomen chose to additionally undergo a penectomy to remove their penises, although doing so greatly reduces their chances of having a vaginaplasty successfully performed later in life.

Reassignment surgery for transmen, while having made great advancements in recent years, still has not reached the same level of success that male-to-female reassignment surgery has. Female-to-male gender reassignment surgical options currently[21] include hysterectomy, vaginectomy, salpingo-oophorectomy, metoidoplasty, scrotoplasty, urethroplasty, placement of testicular prostheses and phalloplasty.

The simplest gender reassignment procedure for a transman is a metoidoplasty, a procedure that takes advantage of the fact that testosterone therapy often triggers a considerable increase in size of the clitoris. During a metoidoplasty, a surgeon surgically releases the clitoral tendons and moves the clitoris to a more forward position. This procedure creates a small, sexually sensate penis that can become naturally erect. A transman can chose to augment a metoidoplasty with an urethroplasty, a procedure that extends the urethra using tissue typically harvested from the cheeks of the mouth or from the vaginal

_____

[21] Circa 2009

area. Extending the urethra allows a surgeon to relocate the urethral opening to its anatomically correct location at the tip of the penis.

The advantages to a metoidoplasty are that the resulting penis is erotically sensate, can naturally engorge, and if the penis is long enough, can be use to penetrate a partner. A transman who undergoes both a metoidoplasty and urethroplasty should also be able to urinate while standing upon completion of both procedures.

The major disadvantage of a metoidoplasty is that the constructed penis is often so small that a transman cannot effectively penetrate a partner with it. Extending the urethra through the penis to its anatomically correct location at the tip also incurs the risk that the urethral extension at some time will tear or come apart within the penis, possibly leading to infection and penile tissue death.

As an alternative to a metoidoplasty, a transman can choose to undergo a phalloplasty to construct a penis that is considerably longer and thicker than the penis that results from undergoing a metoidoplasty. In a phalloplasty, surgeons use skin and subcutaneous tissues taken from other parts of the body such as the abdomen, groin, leg, side of the torso, forearm, etc. to create a penis that is large enough to penetrate a partner during sex. There are a quite a number of phalloplasty variations, each of which uses different techniques to create the penis.

A phalloplasty may require the implantation of a pump device that allows the transman to manually inflate / engorge the penis prior to engaging in sex. Alternatively, the penis constructed during a phalloplasty procedure may have an opening that allows for the insertion of a flexible rod to increase the rigidity of the penis. As with a metoidoplasty, a surgeon can perform an urethroplasty in conjunction with a phalloplasty, although the risk of complications is much higher due to the increase in length of the urethral extension that the surgeon must create.

A phalloplasty can have several significant disadvantages that include the construction of penis that is not realistic in appearance, which is not sexually sensate, which does not naturally engorge, and which is prone to damage during sex. Additionally, several of the phalloplasty surgical variations come with high risks of tissue death, leave extensive scarring on one or more visible parts of the body, and can lead to the formation of strictures and fistulas. Phalloplasty also carries with it a risk of nerve damage in the areas from which the tissue used to create the penis originates, resulting in the possibility of permanent loss of sensation or function in those areas.

A transman can also choose to undergo several additional surgical procedures as part of his gender reassignment. He may choose to remove his uterus, ovaries and / or vagina, and have the vaginal opening closed. He may also undergo a scrotoplasty, a procedure in which silicone testicular implants are placed inside hollowed labia majora, and the labia majora are then joined together to form a scrotum.

Although transwomen and transmen both risk the loss of sexual function or other debilitating complications as an unintended result of having undergone reassignment surgery, the probability that a serious problem will occur as a result of GRS is much higher for transmen. Because of the very high risk of complications, the numerous surgical procedures that transmen must endure to change gender, and the extremely high financial costs associated with gender reassignment, many transmen simply forego reassignment surgery altogether and opt to only remove their ovaries and uteruses. Although this does not give them genitals that are congruent with their gender identities, it does relieve them of their monthly menstrual cycles and halts the production of female hormones within their bodies. So while their gender dysphoria may not be completely relieved, it may be significantly reduced by undergoing these limited surgical procedures.

Regardless of how one identifies, gender reassignment surgery has many negative drawbacks that everyone contemplating gender reassignment surgery must evaluate and reflect upon. For a young transsexual, reassignment surgery usually removes the possibility of naturally parenting a child. If the transitioning person wishes to create a directly descendant family sometime later in life, he or she must harvest and preserve sperm or eggs for future in-vitro fertilization prior to starting hormone replacement therapy[22]. Transsexuals who do not plan for a future family, and who want to establish a family later in life, may need to turn to adoption for children. Discrimination, sadly, can make adoption an unavailable option for transsexuals, possibly leaving a transsexual and his or her partner childless.

Reassignment surgery also permanently removes the organs that produce hormones necessary for a healthy life. Both transmen and transwomen may have problems with weak bones earlier in life than natal women and men. Long-term use of hormones such as testosterone, estrogen and progesterone may lead to liver damage, blood clots, early heart disease and cancer. Medical science is currently unsure whether hormone replacement therapy is safe or not, so the decision to undergo reassignment surgery may come with great future health risks.

In the end though, many transsexuals find the emotional pain that arises from having an incongruent gender identity generally trumps all the risks associated with gender reassignment surgery. They accept the recommended solution for severe gender dysphoria, which is to change one's sex to match one's gender identity. While dangerous and risky, reassignment surgery is a risk many people are willing to accept to bring peace and joy to their lives.

Please take sufficient time to contemplate the surgical procedures you may undertake to find peace in your life. Just as saying "I think I'm transsexual" cannot be unsaid, a surgeon cannot restore a penis, vagina, uterus, breast or any other body part that you decide to have surgically removed. Deciding to undergo gender reassignment surgery can bring

---

[22] Long-term hormone replacement therapy may cause permanent sterility in transsexuals. Although this is not a certainty in every case, you should collect sperm or eggs while healthy, as viable specimens can be safely collected and stored.

great joy to your life or leave you miserable if you wrongly undertake the surgical path. Be sure to talk openly and honestly with your counselors, be honest with yourself, and make decisions that are right for you and only you. **Remember this is your unique journey, unlike any other transsexual's journey, and whether your journey takes you through the surgical suite is only something you can decide.**

TRANSITIONING AND RELIGION

Almost everyone has strong beliefs regarding the existence of God, whether God should be honored and worshipped if She does exist, and whether an organized religion is the best way to honor God. Transitioning can, in its unique way, change you with respect to all three of these beliefs.

"How can a god exist that allows a person to have a gender identity which does not match his or her sex?" "Why should I love a god that made me this way?" These are questions I have heard more than once, and I am sure will be uttered for eons to come. These are also the questions that expose how much hurt really exists inside of you if you are transgender.

I cannot definitively prove that God exists. I believe She does for reasons I do not wish to explain here. You may not agree with me, though, if you have lived your life with a gender identity that does not match your sex. You may have experienced feelings of extreme loneliness, being truly alone in the universe, being a mistake of nature, being a reject, or not being loved by God. You may have believed that no god could exist that would allow you to be the way you are.

Regardless of whether you transition or not, you are not alone. Other transgender people experience the same feelings of loneliness as you. Do not lose hope. I strongly believe that having an incongruent gender identity is a natural variation that occurs in nature, like any of the other variations in nature that God allows to exist, however cruel, seemingly difficult to comprehend, or unusual they may be.

Transitioning may awaken you to several concepts about yourself that you may have never accepted before. You may find self-esteem, inner strength and great inner pride. You may realize that you are a good human being. You may realize that you can address your condition through a number of means, one of which is transitioning. You may come to the realization that there is no reason God picked you to be on this incredibly hard journey, you are just on it.

And when you realize that your condition, the condition of being born with an incongruent gender identity, is not a punishment of God or a scourge that She placed upon you for reasons you cannot fathom, you may just believe in God once again. You may come to believe that God needs to be worshipped or thanked for the gifts She has given you.

There may be times following the great hardships of transition that you will sit down and find yourself thanking God for allowing you the strength, health and courage to overcome the extreme obstacle you just conquered. I know that when I stepped into my own bedroom after having returned from facial feminization surgery, I felt an incredible thankfulness to God for allowing me to have lived through the extreme surgery that I had just undergone. When I dilated[23] myself for the first time following gender reassignment surgery, I thanked God for allowing me to finally have the proper genitals. When my parents, sisters, brother, daughters and friends kept me in their lives, I felt an incredible thankfulness to God for placing such good, loving people in my life.

Even if you do not believe God exists, some of the experiences of transitioning may make you question your beliefs. I am not saying this will certainly happen, but in some lonely moment immediately before a surgery or coming out to a family member, you may find yourself praying to a god you did not believe exists. Do not underestimate the emotional journey you will make as you transition. It truly is incredible.

---

[23] Vaginal dilation is a procedure that a post-operative transwoman performs to ensure that her vagina does not shrink in depth or circumference over time. A post-operative transwoman should dilate herself several times a week for the rest of her life in order to properly maintain her vagina.

If you worship God as a member of an organized religion, you may unfortunately find yourself an outcast of that religion as you transition. Many religions believe transitioning is an abomination of God's laws or that religion's basic religious tenets. Many other religions believe being transgender is a perversion or a sin, or they believe that surgery does not or will not modify a person's gender.

You may find that an unintended consequence of transitioning is that your sexual orientation may not change, making you a gay man or a lesbian after your reassignment surgery is complete. For some religions, however, being gay is even worse than being transgender or transsexual. Hence, if you were not outcast when the other members of your place of worship learned that you are transgender, you may be outcast when they find you to be a gay or a lesbian at the end of your transition.

Being cast aside, thrown away, or hated by your religion may make you seriously reconsider your desire to be a member of any organized religion. Even if your religion does not cast you out, you may lose your desire to be a member of your religion when you realize many of the doctrines of your religion directly conflict with your own beliefs.

You may feel anger and hatred toward your religion when you no longer feel that you are free to fully practice your beliefs. This may strongly diminish your desire to participate in any organized religion for years or decades to come.

However, variations exist in religions just as variations naturally occur in nature. Some research on your part may lead you to religions that accept transgenderism as being natural, and which do not see transitioning as being an abomination of God's law. Research may also show you that there are places of worship within your current religion that are far more tolerant and accepting of transgender people than others, allowing you to retain your religion through and after the transition process. Do not give up hope of finding a new place to worship if you suddenly find yourself alone in a spiritual sense.

If you are uncertain whether a specific place of worship will accept you or not, go talk with the leader of the place of worship you wish to attend. See if he or she is prejudiced or open minded, and see if he or she will accept you with open arms into the religious community that you wish to join. If he or she is not willing to accept you if you move forward with your transition, most likely neither will the rest of the congregation.

If you need to be a member of an organized religion, do not give up hope. There are religions that accept transsexuals. And if you gave up hope on organized religions years ago, do not be surprised if the journey you are on leads you to seek a place where you can thank God for being alive and being able to conquer the incredible burden of being transgender.

TRUE ACCEPTANCE

No transwoman wants people to call her by her former name in public. Neither does a transman ever want someone calling him a she. Obviously, to do so is embarrassing and will draw attention to either the transgender person, or the person using the wrong name or pronoun.

However, when you are talking privately with someone in your family such as your mother or father, should you allow them to call you by your birth name or refer to you by your birth gender? For just about everyone I met who was transitioning, the answer to this question is a resounding "No." Usage of the new name and gender-appropriate pronouns is a very important issue, even from family members.

Sometimes people make the mistake of using a former name or the wrong pronouns just out of habit. Take a second and consider how hard it would be for you if one of your best friends changed his or her first name. It would be terribly hard for you to never use the old name ever again. I am sure, though, that you would try. You may get it wrong at first, but you would try and possibly correct yourself when you said the wrong name. Therefore, when you first come out to family and friends, you need to make considerations for the lifetime in which they knew you by your former name and gender. They are only human, and they need time to consciously change how they refer to you.

Eventually, however, everyone including family members should adapt to your new name, especially if you legally changed your name. When months or years go by and people still call you by your former name, there may be a more significant underlying reason other than forgetfulness or habit. The person who is using your former name or gender may be doing so because he or she refuses to accept you in your new gender.

You may find this confusing as your family and friends may have acted well towards you since you came out to them. They did not run and hide, nor did they throw you out with the bath water. They still talk with you and show you love and concern. However, not rejecting someone is different from truly accepting that person.

After you come out to all the people in your life, the period that follows is also a transition period for each person that you told. You are not the only person transitioning. Everyone that you have come out to must also make their own psychological and emotional journey, in which they forget the image of the old you and start to accept you in your new gender.

Simply put, it is going to take a long time for most people to make their journeys and to accept you fully. Imagine how hard it would be for you to accept your sister as your brother if she was transitioning. It would be incredibly hard to forget the little girl you grew up with, or the girl who may have been a bridesmaid in your wedding. And so it is just as hard for your family and friends when you come out to them. Your message to them is "I'm just changing my sex, that's all." The message they get, though, is "I'm no longer your son, I'm your daughter", or "I'm no longer your sister, I'm your brother", or "I'm not your husband, I'm your wife".

You may be hurt when your brother calls you "bro" instead of "sis" a year after you came out to him. Besides being hurt, you are going to be angry and frustrated, because in your mind you may believe a year is more than enough time for your brother to get it straight. When this occurs, you are going to have to step back and realize you are wishing to be truly accepted, and true acceptance may be very long in coming, if it ever comes at all.

Once transsexuals start to make their transitions and begin to live full-time, they do not ever want anyone to see them as their old selves, call them by their old names, or refer to them by their old genders. They just want the world to accept them fully as members of their new gender. Making the world forget the old you is not as easy as you would wish. Hence, you will never entirely fulfill your desire to have everyone truly accept you. That is a hard nut to swallow.

Dealing with the emotional stress caused by not gaining true acceptance from family and true friends is very hard to do by yourself. This is why I think counseling on how to handle the desire for true acceptance is the third most important role of a therapist. Most likely, you are not going to see the actions of your family as acceptance issues. You are probably going to see your family and friends as being stubborn, hateful, or controlling. Talking with them directly about proper name or pronoun usage may not make anything better as it is going to take time and healing for them to let the "old you" go. They may also not be able to express very well how much it hurts to have to call you "she", considering they knew and loved you for what seemed like forever as "he".

True acceptance takes both time and exposure. The more people have a chance to interact with you in your new gender, the more they will become accustomed to treating and referring to you properly. People you do not deal with regularly enough are just going to have too little stimulus to truly accept you. They may not reject you, but they will not truly accept you either.

Some people, though, are just stubborn, zealots or hateful. They may not have ostracized you when you came out, but in their own minds, they do not ever have to accept you as a member of your new gender. My advice is that people like this simply have to be avoided or marginalized in your life if possible, as they do much more harm than good.

Although it is going to be hard for you to do, there may be times during your transition when you may have to lose someone important to you, such as a family member or friend, as a result of you walking away from him or her. Typically we worry about coming out to someone and having them abandon us, but there are times when it is necessary to abandon others who just cannot truly accept a transsexual person, and intentionally act in either a hurtful or demeaning manner whenever they are around one.

If you do walk away from someone, do not lock the door and throw away the key. They may find it in their hearts one day to change and accept you. If they do so without placing conditions on your transition or gender expression, you should consider overlooking the hurt and pain they caused you. It is not always easy to take the high road in a relationship, but the rewards can be very satisfying when things are finally back in order. You do not have to accept anyone back into your life that hurt you, but try to keep in the back of your mind that it was you that came out to them, forcing a huge burden upon them. Therefore, you should be willing to make some effort to forget about the past when they are ready to unconditionally accept you in your identified gender.

Seek professional help if the stress of not being truly accepted becomes too overpowering, especially during the holidays or on special occasions. It is so easy to lose hope when your parents say they will never be able to love you in your new gender, you do not get invited to family events, or your kids refuse to be seen publicly with you. Transitioning is much harder than just modifying your body. Transitioning subjects you to incredible emotional stresses that can often require counseling or medication to overcome.

SEX AND RELATIONSHIPS

Gender identity, sex, and sexual orientation are individually unique facets of each person. Changing one facet does not necessarily change another. Contrary to popular beliefs, transitioning does not always result in a change of sexual orientation. In general, post-operative transsexuals remain sexually attracted to people of the gender they were attracted to before they transitioned.

This generalization holds true for most, if not all, transsexuals. An example of this is a transman whom others labeled as a butch lesbian prior to transitioning. While living as a woman prior to the transition, *she* was attracted to women and regularly had sex with them. After undergoing reassignment surgery and a double mastectomy, he found that he is still attracted to women. As before, he only has sexual relations with women. Those around him now label him as being a heterosexual man although his sexual orientation did not change.

For some, though, a change in sexual behavior occurs after a transition, but the sexual orientation itself does not change. This creates an appearance of change in the sexual orientation, although a change did not actually occur.

To make sense of this, consider the case of a middle-aged transwoman who while living as a male prior to the transition was in a normal husband / wife relationship. *He* always knew that *he* was more attracted to men than he was to women, but *he* was always too scared to enter into a gay relationship[24]. To the world, though, *he* appeared heterosexual before transitioning. After the transition from male to

---

[24] Prior to transitioning, this person could be classified as being a closeted gay male.

female, she became free to start acting on her natural attraction towards men. People around her suddenly saw her as having a change in her sexual orientation but in reality, the only thing that changed was her sexual behavior. She secretly liked men before transitioning, and now, she is having sex with men in heterosexual relationships[25].

As another example, take the case of a transwoman who has always been very much attracted to women[26]. Following GRS, she finds she is still attracted to women, but finds it very frustrating trying to meet a lesbian who is attracted to her in the small town she lives in. She realizes that some of the men in town are attracted to her, and she thinks some of them are kind. She happens to meet a guy who finds her attractive, who treats her well and she finds that she enjoys his friendship. Although she is not truly sexually attracted to him, she starts into a sexual relationship with him. To everyone around her, she appears to be heterosexual after transitioning but secretly is still very much attracted to women[27].

For a few transsexuals, though, sexual orientation may change after a transition. Hormone therapy, newfound open mindedness, ability to have and enjoy sexual relations in the new gender, experimentation, etc. allow people of the gender that was never previously sexually attractive to suddenly become sexually attractive after a transition.

What will your sexual orientation and behavior be after you complete your transition? The simple answer often said is "Only you know the answer to that question." However, I believe the more accurate answer is to say that even you are not going to know whom you are attracted to, or whom you will be sexually active with, until you complete your transition. Time, hormones, experiences,

---

[25] After transitioning, people label this person a heterosexual woman.

[26] Prior to the transition, people label this person a heterosexual male.

[27] Although people label this person a heterosexual woman, she is secretly a closeted lesbian.

experimentation, ability to pass and be seen as attractive, sexual compatibility, etc. are all going to have an influence on whether or not you perceive members of a particular gender to be sexually desirable or not.

As time goes by, you may find yourself having sexual thoughts and feelings that you did not previously consider possible. This may shock and confuse you to say the least. However, if you look at these new thoughts and feeling in a positive way, being transsexual has given you the opportunity to grow beyond the restrictions you grew up with concerning sexual orientation and relations. Not too many people get to experience making love from both sides of the fence.

Regardless of your sexual orientation after transition, you may find yourself the subject of discrimination or harassment even if you consider yourself heterosexual after transition. In western culture, people in general are very critical of other people's sexual orientation. People assign almost everyone a label according to his or her perceived[28] sexual orientation: lesbian, gay, bi-sexual, heterosexual, etc. Transsexuals, though, can find that they may be simultaneously assigned conflicting and opposite sexual orientation labels, based not upon their actual sexual orientation, but based instead upon the misguided beliefs concerning transsexuals in general.

Take for instance the case of a post-operative transwoman who is in a relationship with a pre-operative transwoman. Both transwomen's sexual attraction is towards women, and the post-operative transwoman is willing to overlook the fact her partner, whom she sees as a woman, still has male plumbing while she transitions. In their own eyes, they each see themselves as lesbians. People around them who accept them as women also see them as lesbians. A good portion of the

---

[28] Labels are often applied based solely on perceptions, not facts. People often label effeminate men as being gay and butch women as being lesbians solely because of how they express their gender, and without any regard to their actual sexual preferences.

population, however, refuses to accept any pre-operative transsexual as the gender with which he or she identifies and presents. For these people, the couple is heterosexual because the post-op transwoman has female genitalia and the pre-op transwoman still has male genitalia. Further confusing the matter, a portion of the population refuses to recognize that reassignment surgery actually changes a person's sex. For this group of people, the couple is gay regardless of their genitals because they both were born male and have male DNA.

So what does this truly mean for a transsexual? It means that as a transsexual you will always be a potential target for discriminating comments and actions regardless of with whom you are in a relationship. If a transsexual presents well and shows affection publicly for someone of the opposite sex (e.g. a transwoman kissing a man), there will probably be very little reaction from those around them, as this appears to be heterosexual behavior in most parts of the world. However, if the transsexual presents poorly or shows affection for someone of the same sex (e.g. a transwoman kissing a genetic woman, or a transwoman who does not pass well embracing a man), there may be bad reactions from those around them as this may appear to be a lesbian or gay act.

The members of the lesbian and gay community sadly know that there are places where society tolerates their public displays of affection, also known as PDAs, and places where society does not. Each transsexual also has to make that same determination of where he or she can show affection, and where he or she cannot.

You may be thinking to yourself that this is just insane and you will do whatever pleases you. Well that is a great belief if you live in a large, liberal, American or European city. However, there are locations worldwide where people do not tolerate the outward display of what is perceived to be gay or lesbian affection. As a result, you and your partner may be putting yourselves in harm's way for doing something as simple as kissing or holding hands in public. Hate-motivated crimes occur even in the large cities that people think of being liberal. Please do not let the consequences of your affections become motivation for a new hate crimes law!

If you have not realized it already, transitioning requires a person be thick skinned. You will learn over time to ignore and handle other people's opinions of you. However, there is one opinion regarding the perception of your sexual orientation, however, that is critical and which you cannot discount: your own. It may not make a difference to you in the least if you go from being in heterosexual relationships prior to transitioning to being in same-sex relationships post-transition. On the other hand, if you suddenly realize that you are gay, lesbian, bi-sexual or straight for that matter, this sudden realization may very well become an issue that you are ill prepared to handle. Seek professional help if your sexual orientation and behavior concerns become an issue for you after your transition.

Regardless of your sexual orientation, there are some questions regarding relationships that only time and experience will provide the answers. Will you be able to establish friendships and develop relationships? Will family, friends or co-workers discriminate against you because of your choice of partner? If you find you have same-sex interests, will members of the LGB community discriminate against you because you are transsexual?

Hopefully you will find that establishing a relationship post-transition is done pretty much the same way everyone else establishes a relationship. All relationships require a certain amount of physical and emotional attraction, and being a transwoman or a transman who is establishing a relationship is no different. You and the person you have interests in both must have a physical attraction towards each other, and you both must connect with each other on some personal, emotional level. There are, however, some caveats to this rule.

The first caveat is that you are going to have to be honest and open with your new love very early on in the relationship about your transgender status and history. This is for personal safety, honesty and trust reasons. Your disclosure, though, may cause the person whom you have interests in to walk away from the relationship. As unfortunate as this may be, it is desirable for a breakup to occur earlier rather than later if a breakup does occur due to your disclosure of your past. If you establish a relationship on falsities, the relationship will most likely fail at some later point in time. All the effort you put into building that relationship will be lost.

The second caveat is that the person you have eyes for must be a bit more naturally tolerant than a person who enters into a non-trans relationship. A perspective partner must be strong enough to ward off any prejudice that he or she may encounter by being the partner of a transsexual. He or she must be willing to overlook some personal traits of your birth gender that you exhibit from time to time. In addition, he or she must be willing to overlook the physical differences of your body that are artifacts of your birth sex or surgeries when you disrobe.

Another caveat is that there has to be a consideration made for post-transition sexual compatibility. While there have been great advancements in surgical techniques over the years, not all people who undergo reassignment surgery will have sexual organs that are as fully functional and capable as their genetic sisters or brothers. If you are a transwoman, your vagina may not be deep enough or wide enough to accommodate the man you want as your partner. If you are a transman, your may have very little sexual sensation during intercourse. You and your perspective partner are going to have to communicate well, and find alternative means of pleasuring each other if you have physical compatibility limitations.

Finally, if you and your partner get serious enough to consider entering into a civil union or marriage, you and your partner will have to consider your inability to naturally conceive children. Depending upon the type of reassignment surgery you undergo, you may end up becoming sterile, and this may become an issue at some point in the relationship. Artificial insemination and adoption are ways to get around this problem for many people, but there always remains the possibility that your partner may not want to parent a child that does not naturally result from the union or marriage.

With all of these concerns, are there really women or men who are capable of accepting you as a partner after you tell them you are or were transsexual? The answer is definitely "yes". Not everyone you meet or set your sites upon will be open or tolerant enough to establish a relationship with a transsexual person, but there are definitely some that will. Like all other personal relationships, the amount of physical and emotional attraction your potential partner has for you will play a major role in determining which aspects that a possible partner will be willing to overlook and compensate for.

Although it may not be immediately obvious, a certain subset of people may find transsexuals more desirable than "regular" people. The slight differences in body shapes, height, strength, personal knowledge and experiences may be just what someone finds especially attractive in a partner.

When it comes to meeting people with the intent of establishing a new relationship, you are just going to have to get out in public and start socializing. This may be hard to do depending on your own self-confidence level, your ability to pass and most importantly your attitude. A positive, friendly attitude goes such a long way when you are trying to meet people. A smile can substitute for a thousand words. Being open and welcoming will make people want to be around you.

What I am saying here is nothing new; you have to be attractive to a potential partner in more ways than physical beauty in order to catch his or her eye.

So, maybe you have met someone special during your transition and you feel it is time that you try to become sexually involved. Moving from a platonic relationship to a sexual relationship can be a traumatic experience for both parties for a number of reasons. For a pre-op transwoman, anti-androgen medications such as spironolactone and hormones such as estradiol can limit sexual desire and the ability to perform sexually. She may additionally get the feeling she is being assigned a male sex role, and she may feel "dirty" or "unnatural" having anal sex performed on her by a genetic male or a transman prior to undergoing reassignment surgery. Similarly, a transman may feel as if he is being assigned a female sex role if he is relations with a partner who wishes to penetrate him vaginally prior to reassignment surgery.

Other body image problems may impede both transmen and transwomen. A partner may feel awkward about being with a pre-operative transwomen who still has male genitalia, or a pre- or post-operative transman who still has female genitalia. People are fickle about their sexual partners, and being transsexual increases the number of things that can make them more selective or difficult to satisfy.

Simply put, many things can go wrong while trying to establish a sexual relationship during and after the transition process. There is not an easy way to predict whether problems will arise between two people, but couples will probably have the best chance of being sexually happy if they are both completely honest and open with each other about their fears, concerns, and desires before they undress in the bedroom for the first time.

If you overcome the fear of the bedroom before undergoing GRS, there is another consideration that may pop up as the date for reassignment surgery approaches. Is the non-trans person in the relationship going to be capable of remaining involved after the reassignment surgery? Just maybe the girl you believe to be a lesbian really likes the fact that you have a face like a girl, have breasts like a girl, can publicly be her girlfriend, and still have male genitalia to provide that little something extra at the end of an evening of sexual fun. Will she be happy that you are physically a woman following surgery, or will she be disappointed that you can no longer have intercourse with her? You may want to discuss this with her before you get into a sexual relationship, or before you commit to a date for surgery. You may be returning to an empty bedroom if you do not.

My second therapist offered to me what I considered to be good advice concerning my desire to get into a relationship while I was transitioning. "Don't!" When you evaluate the complexities, problems, and general crapola that accompany transitioning, getting into a relationship, especially a sexual relationship, is just like adding fuel to a fire. There exists a good chance you are going to be scorched or burnt. Make sure you are truly emotionally ready before you head into a relationship. Although being loved and giving love are such wonderful things, a relationship during the transition process can add incredible stress to your life regardless of whether the relationship is good or bad. Maybe transitioning should be that point in life during which you just quietly tolerate having a single lifestyle.

However, maybe it is not; transitions vary wildly from person to person. It is not fair to think someone should be without a partner or a love interest for possibly a decade or more if that is how long it takes to go through the transition process. Like everything else in a transition, dating and being in a relationship is something that you will have to evaluate as being a good or bad thing for your unique journey. If you find someone whom you love, and who loves you in return, then embrace that relationship if you feel it is the right thing for you to do.

In summary, give some thought as to whether or not you really need to be in a close, personal relationship as you transition. Maybe a good group of friends will help satisfy your friendship needs. If you find yourself in a very close and deeply personal relationship, make sure you talk honestly and openly with your partner before you attempt to move the relationship from the living room, to the bedroom. When you go for reassignment surgery, make sure you and your partner are both ready for this change. Never forget to be safe. Do not fall victim to a stranger who is upset by your displays of public affection or by a surprised sexual partner. Lastly, if you can overcome the burden imposed by transitioning on a relationship, genuinely care for, and always respect your partner. Do not forget he or she is human and has his or her own wants, needs, desires and fears. Do not allow your transition to overshadow the relationship you build or your partner's needs.

FINDING PEACE

Prior to seeking professional help for my gender dysphoria, I lived my life in such a manner that almost no one would ever detect I was in any way different from any other average man. I built incredible defenses around myself to protect my image of masculinity in an attempt to shield myself from ridicule for being too effeminate. I wanted others to like me, and so I tried to be what I thought everyone around me expected me to be.

Nothing that I did prior to transitioning relieved me of the pain that grew inside of me as the years of my life silently slipped away. Nothing I did reduced my yearning to live the life I knew should have been mine, but was not, for a reason that only God knew. I kept locked inside myself the contempt I felt for being male, never sharing with friends or family my need to change. However, I knew I needed to change my life to make the pain go away. It took a long time, but I eventually realized that internal peace would never come to me while the life that I was living was a lie.

In September 2005, I took that first step towards finding peace in my life when I found the courage to tell my wife that I thought I might be transsexual. Emotionally, it was a huge step for me to bring myself to the point of being able to express my true feelings to another person for the first time in my life. Coming out to my wife also triggered the end of my marriage and ushered in some of the hardest periods of my life. If peace was going to come to my life, it was not going to come easily.

It took a while to realize that internal peace was something that I had to obtain over time. Foremost, I needed to come to grips with who I was. With the help of my first therapist and friend, Cathi Coulson, I found inner strength I did not know I had, and I learned to accept that I was a good person regardless of the fact that I had an incongruent gender identity.

Unfortunately, fears of my birth family disowning me soon eclipsed the peace I found through self-acceptance. I knew I had to tell my parents and siblings that I was transgender and that I was considering a transition, but the thought of having no one in my life that I could call family completely overwhelmed me at the time. I knew there was only one way to overcome this fear, and that meant I had to tell the people I loved.

In January 2006, I walked through Manhattan with my oldest sister Patty, hoping to God she would not abandon me as I uttered, "I think I'm transsexual." to her. Her love for me was strong, and she found the courage within herself to support me that cold afternoon. With the knowledge that there would be one person in my life whom I could call family if I transitioned, I decided that I could transition and hopefully bring an end to my lifelong emotional pain.

The next twenty-one months were a blur of transition tasks: electrolysis; coming out to friends, family and co-workers; voice lessons; a name change; hormone therapy; a legal separation; facial surgeries; counseling; starting the Real-Life Experience; coming out at work; etc. My emotions were like a roller coaster, fifteen minutes up and fifteen minutes down. I was so happy one moment and so terrified the next. In retrospect, I am not sure how I survived. But not only did I survive; I flourished and became happier overall. I was finding peace, but I was also too busy transitioning to notice.

My transition journey eventually brought me to a transgender conference in Atlanta where I met many wonderful people. Something about my presence triggered many of the other transgender people in attendance to share with me their transition stories and their problems. Each of those discussions, however, exposed a little part of my life that I had bottled up and hidden away in some dark corner of my mind: the pain of growing up transgender; the fears that I would lose everyone whom I loved, my job and my home if I transitioned; the apprehension of not knowing what my face would look like after facial feminization surgery; the terror of venturing into public as a woman; the sadness of having two marriages shattered by my gender problems; the countless nights that I fell asleep hoping in the morning that I would awaken as a girl.

After days of sharing the stories and experiences of my life, an incredible, almost spiritual feeling came over me. In sharing my stories, I was forcing myself to reflect upon my life and the pain I had endured for so long. So, at 4:30 AM on the night of my 46th birthday, and a very special birthday at that, I shared some incredible, personal thoughts with my very good friend Jenna. I then broke down and cried for several hours.

For this was the first time that I realized that my wish, really the impossible dream that I dreamt my entire life, had actually come true. My transition had so consumed me that I had not noticed that I had overcome the gender obstacles in my life that were causing all of my emotional pain. I suddenly realized that I had become the woman whom I always wanted to be. The pain in my life had gone away, and I was the happiest I had ever been. Everyone, even people who had never met me before, could feel the aura of happiness I was putting off. They sought me out like moths seeking a flame. Then it finally dawned on me what I had been missing.

Even though my gender reassignment surgery was still nine months away, and technically, I had not finished the physical transition, I realized in those early morning hours as the sun was preparing to rise over Atlanta, that I had mentally completed my transition. More importantly, though, I realized that I had finally made peace with my life, my gender, and myself. It was truly an incredible feeling.

I strongly believe now that finding inner peace should be the primary goal of everyone who has an incongruent gender identity, and who suffers internally as a result of living his or her life in the wrong gender. Undergoing reassignment surgery, learning to pass, etc. are just some of the many challenges we take on to make the pain go away on the road to finding our inner peace. However, these tasks are just milestones on the journey, never the destination. You should never measure your transition by whether you have completed one of these milestones or not. **Your transition, which is a unique experience for you, will be a success *only* when you find inner peace.**

You will find thru experience that transitioning comes with many costs, some of which can cause severe emotional distress. Transitioning also carries with it many great hardships, physical pain, and at times, great sorrows. A poorly executed or failed transition can destroy a life. Never forget that a transition that leaves you in an emotional state of mind that is worse than the state of mind you were in before your transition is not a success.

If after considering all the benefits and hardships that may result if you transition you feel you could possibly be in a worse place emotionally or physically than when you started, you should seriously reconsider your plans to transition, and you should look for other means of finding peace in your life. You should only start your transition when you feel that you can progress to some point in which you will be at peace with yourself, your gender, and the way you live your life. Do not rush foolishly into your transition. Plan carefully. Do not skip steps that will come back to haunt you later.

When you have decided that you want to take the chance, and follow the long, dark, and unimaginably difficult road that starts with the utterance of "I think I'm transsexual." to someone you love, I wish you luck on your journey. I hope that by undertaking this incredibly hard commitment and transformation, you find a cure to the gender dysphoria that has haunted you throughout your life. Most of all, I hope you find peace within yourself and in your life.

- Mara

AFTERTHOUGHTS (*EPILOGUE*)

A friend of mine asked me one evening what life was like now that I have completed my transition. It took a while for me to express my feelings to her. After I told her, she expressed the thought that many of the people who are considering a transition might have no idea of what to expect after the physical transition is complete, and I should consider adding my experiences to this guide.

Although I consider my post-operative experiences not to be part of a guide on how to transition, here are a few reflections on my life after reassignment surgery. I hope your post-operative experiences will be as good as or even better than my own!

For me, the answer to the question "What is life like after transition?" is "It just feels right!" I do not have any feeling of loss or sadness as a result of transitioning. What I have instead is an incredible feeling that my body is finally proper. When I walk nude in front of a full-length mirror, I feel content and happy. I know that not everything is perfect with my appearance as I am much taller than the average woman, but that does not matter all that much in the grand scheme of things. I feel very good inside.

A lot of the time, though, I feel I should answer the "What is life like after transition?" question by trying to explain what I no longer feel instead of what I am feeling. I no longer have the pervasive feeling that my gender is wrong. For me, the gender dysphoria is a fading memory. I find it hard to explain this feeling of lack of dysphoria to people who have never felt a dissonance between their gender and gender identity. It is similar to trying to explain what it is like to no longer be feeling pain to someone who has never experienced pain.

I am surprised sometimes that I am so at peace with the results of my reassignment surgeries. I rather expected before having undergone

GRS that I would have some type of feeling of loss after the surgery, but there just has not been any such feeling. There is no sense of loss, only a feeling of completion. I feel very much at peace with the results, my body, and my life.

Regarding my sexuality, I feel that I am an attractive woman now. My surgical results far exceeded my wildest dreams. I feel that there are people who are sexually attracted to me as a woman, and this gives me a feeling of pride. I feel comfortable with my post-operative body, and I know that if I choose to be with someone I care about in the future, he or she will see me as a woman both with and without my clothes on.

I have not completely figured out what my sexual orientation is and to whom I am attracted. I know I am still primarily attracted to women, but I find myself at random times attracted to men. This is scary in many ways as I never have been with a man, but in some strange way, it feels surprisingly natural to think about being with a man now that I am physically female. I will just have to see where this new road that I am on leads me. My journey is far from over, and I am very much, still enjoying the trip.

On occasion, I still find myself feeling scared and apprehensive. I feel that being transsexual is an 800 lb gorilla lurking in the shadows, waiting to jump in the way of a possibly beautiful relationship with someone I care for deeply. I am afraid of discrimination by those who hate me for being transsexual even though they have never met me. In contrast, I also feel strong, defiant, and proud of who I am. If transitioning has done nothing else for me, it definitely gave me the courage to overcome my greatest fears, and instilled in me an immense sense of self-pride and self-worth.

I feel that I still have much to learn about living as a woman and how to properly interact as a female with others. I am not sure I will ever be able to catch up to genetic women in these areas. This leaves me sometimes feeling like a teenager exploring her world for the first time. At other times, I feel like a confident young woman who thinks she knows how to get what she wants, but in reality does not. And when the reality of my age sets in, I sometimes feel too old to be learning all the lessons that life as a woman wants to teach me. I know, though, that I must keep learning as I make my journey, for there will never be an end to the lessons that this incredible path that I have chosen for my life wishes to teach me.

Overall, I find I am both happy and content at this moment in my life. I feel at peace with myself for possibly the first time ever; a feeling accented by a lack of emotional pain. I have a very strong sense that I am emotionally well.

So would I transition again if I could replay my life from the start? Most definitely yes! I only wish I could have transitioned earlier in my life. However, the hands of time cannot be run backwards, even for me. I am who I am as a result of all that I experienced throughout my life, both male and female, both good and bad. I am distinctly unique and special as a result of the gender synergy that exists within me. I am happy to be me, even if I carry this extra burden of being transsexual.

I no longer dream of being reincarnated as a girl. Instead, I have a persistent sense that when that final moment comes to my life, I can close my eyes, creak out a small, faint smile, and die in peace. My final wishes are for my death certificate to say female like my birth certificate, and to be remembered long after I am gone as a woman.

And finally, "Am I happy now?" Unequivocally "Yes!"